From Words to Gramma.

From Words to Grammar is a different introduction to grammar for students. Taking a word-based approach to grammar, this innovative book introduces the subject through the analysis of over a hundred of the most commonly used English words.

Each unit focuses on a different word class, using an analysis of specific words which includes:

- an introduction to the grammar of each word;
- examples of real world usage featuring that word;
- exercises with answers.

This unique approach not only introduces students to grammar but also provides them with an understanding of how grammar works in everyday English. Written by an experienced teacher and author, *From Words to Grammar* is ideal for all students of English Language.

Roger Berry is the former Head of English at Lingnan University in Hong Kong and has authored four books on English grammar, including *English Grammar: A Resource Book for Students* (2012).

From Words to Grammar

Discovering English Usage

Roger Berry

Routledge
Taylor & Francis Group

LONDON AND NEW YORK

First published 2015
by Routledge
2 Park Square, Milton Park, Abingdon, Oxon OX14 4RN

and by Routledge
711 Third Avenue, New York, NY 10017

Routledge is an imprint of the Taylor & Francis Group, an informa business

© 2015 Roger Berry

British Library Cataloguing-in-Publication Data
A catalogue record for this book is available from the British Library

Library of Congress Cataloging-in-Publication Data
Berry, Roger, 1951–
From words to grammar / Roger Berry.
    pages cm
  Includes index.
  1. English language – Grammar – Programmed instruction.
  2. English language – Grammar – Study and teaching.
  3. Language experience approach in education. I. Title.
  PE1112.5.B47 2015
  428.2–dc23   2014046164

ISBN: 978-0-415-71375-7 (hbk)
ISBN: 978-0-415-71376-4 (pbk)
ISBN: 978-1-315-71256-7 (ebk)

Typeset in Goudy
by HWA Text and Data Management, London
Printed and bound in Great Britain by Ashford Colour Press Ltd, Gosport, Hampshire

MIX
Paper from
responsible sources
FSC
www.fsc.org   FSC® C011748

Contents

Introduction

This book is based on a growing belief among linguists that the grammar of English is much more closely connected to its lexis, or vocabulary, than originally thought. In other words, in addition to learning grammar top-down, i.e. learning the general rules of grammar and applying them to the lexical units systematically, we need to be aware of how individual words work and build up from there. In this way, the book deals with important areas of grammar that general introductions to English grammar do not cover; for example, the behaviour of the individual modal auxiliaries, or of aspect adverbs such as *yet*, *already* and *still*.

The book is divided into twelve chapters, each one dealing with an important area of grammar built around different word classes or sub-classes: nouns, verbs, prepositions, etc. Each chapter starts with a general introduction; this is then followed by a number of sections dealing with the grammar of individual words. After a brief description, there is one activity (occasionally two) based on a set of authentic examples of how the word is used in English.

One hundred and seventeen words are included. One factor in selection is their frequency in English; for example, *of*, *to*, *in*, *that* and *it* are all in the top ten most frequent words in English. Another factor is representativity; words have been chosen as representatives of their class; for example nouns, even if they are not frequent. A third factor is whether a word can be used grammatically in more than one way. An apparently simple word such as *there*, for example, has two distinct uses, which students are very often not aware of. Indeed, one thing that emerges from the activities is how many words have complex grammar, some of them belonging to several word classes (see Chapters 11 and 12 in particular).

The book is aimed at undergraduate students of English as an academic study, and trainee teachers on postgraduate courses. It is not intended for learners of English wishing to 'brush up' their grammar; the activities would largely be too advanced, and the terminology that allows generalisations to be made would not be appropriate.

The aims of the book are to:

- help students understand the importance of words in grammar;
- give a different 'bottom-up' perspective on English grammar;
- fill in gaps in knowledge of particular words;
- create an awareness of how grammar works for future application (see in particular the techniques for analysing concordance lines below).

Introducing concordance lines

If you haven't seen or used concordance lines before – and even if you have – they can seem a little strange; the text is cut in strange places at the beginning and end (in some books in the middle of a word – but not here), and unknown words are scattered throughout. But after some basic explanations and experience they will become familiar.

Selecting and adapting concordance lines

Concordance lines are taken from a corpus (plural 'corpora') – that is, a large collection of texts that are stored electronically. The basic procedure in searching a corpus (using a concordance programme such as Wordsmith) is called KWIC: 'keyword in context'. This will find as many examples as you want of the word (or string of words) that you are interested in (the keyword), surrounded by as much as you want of its context. For some words, e.g. conjunctions, a long context is necessary. The lines are usually presented with the keyword in the centre. However, in this book, while the keyword is in bold, it is not centred; it may be found close to the beginning or end of the line in order to show the context that is necessary.

For the purpose of this book the searches involved 50 or 100 examples of the keywords. These were then thinned out using the criteria mentioned below, while attempting to retain the representative nature of the lines.

Several techniques were applied to make the lines easier to work with:

- Lengthy phrases that were not necessary to understanding the meaning or the grammar were replaced by dots …; these were also used at the start and end of lines to show that the sentence was incomplete.
- Hesitations and repetitions in spoken text were deleted, and basic punctuation (e.g. questions marks) was inserted.
- Lengthy noun phrases that were essential to the grammar of the line were replaced by pronouns placed in square brackets [ ].

Most of the sets of line in the activities were 'right-sorted'; that is, ordered alphabetically according to the word to the right of the keyword. This can make analysis slightly simpler. Sometimes left-sorting is appropriate, to see, for example if a noun is preceded by one of the articles (a/an or the).

Lines that did not make any sense, dealt with unpleasant topics, did not have a full grammatical structure or had obscure cultural allusions were omitted.

Techniques for dealing with concordance lines

(*Note:* words in bold below are covered in the glossary)

Here are some suggestions for ways of analysing concordance lines:

1. *Look at the words around the keyword.* For example, is there an **object noun phrase** following a **verb**? (This would make it **transitive** – but beware: **objects** do not always follow **verbs** directly.) Sometimes an important clue may be several words away from the keyword. What is the relationship between these words and the keyword? Do they 'go together' in some way? This is by far the most important technique. (See Activity A.)

2. *Try replacing the keyword with a synonym.* Sometimes the form of words does not reveal their true grammatical nature. For example, most verbs (those which are **regular**, plus some which are not) do not distinguish between the form of the **past tense** and that of the *-ed* **participle**, and some **irregular** verbs do not distinguish these from the **infinitive** or **present tense** form. (See Activity B.) Replacing the keyword with a word which is used in the same way and which makes more distinctions can help to disambiguate. For example, replacing *that* with *which* can show that it is a **relative pronoun**.

3. *Add some little words.* Expanding a sentence by adding a part of the verb *be* and a pronoun can help to reveal if a verb form is a **past tense** or an *-ed* **participle**. (See Activity C.)

4. *Try moving words around.* Seeing if a word can be moved to different positions in a sentence can be a test of its grammatical status. **Adverbs,** for instance, are particularly free in their placement and this can be a good way of identifying them. (See Activity D.)

5. *Work out the meaning and relate this to the grammar.* There are many examples in this book of words whose meaning and grammar are interconnected. If the grammar changes so does the meaning, and vice versa. So by identifying a different meaning, you may be able to discern a parallel grammatical difference in cases where it is not so obvious. (See Activity E.)

6. *Change the form of the keyword.* This can provide valuable information about the grammar and meaning of a word. Turning a **noun,** for example, into a **plural** tells us whether it is countable ('**count**') or not. Often the meaning of a **noun** is associated with its **count** status (see Chapter 1). (See Activity F.)

7. *Do not be distracted by unknown words.* This is not really a technique for discovering the grammar of words, but it is an important factor when trying to do so, especially with concordance lines, since they should not be simplified to exclude difficult vocabulary. (See Activity G.)

More than one technique may be useful in dealing with a particular set of lines. Indeed, these techniques can be applied to any text, not just concordance lines.

Sample introductory exercises

Activity A

Technique 1: look at the words around the keyword.
Question: how is *after* being used on these lines?
Hint: look especially at the words following *after*.

1. The best colour seems to happen **after** a warm, still Indian summer.
2. The shark was simply **after** a free meal.
3. Wrapped up in the everyday business of looking **after** her newborn baby, Belinda felt fine.
4. All charges listed in this leaflet may be subject to change **after** publication.
5. We may need to treat your tummy with something else **after** that.
6. Yes, **after** we had given up all intention of going there, we arrived.

Comment

Directly following *after* on lines 1, 2 and 3 there is a group of words (*a warm, still Indian summer / a free meal / her newborn baby*) that we call a **noun phrase.** In 4 and 5 there is a single word following (*publication, that*) which can be regarded as equivalent to a **noun phrase.** Afterwards there is a full stop or a comma; so, we can group the use of *after* on lines 1 to 5 under the same heading. (We call it a **preposition** here; see Chapter 5 for more on the use of **prepositions.**) Line 6 is different; the following words begin with *we* and then a **verb** (*had given*); this is called a **clause** rather than a **noun phrase,** and the name for words that introduce clauses is **conjunction** (see Chapter 12). The terms are not important at the moment, so long as you can identify the different ways in which *after* is used.

Activity B

Technique 2: replace the keyword with a synonym.
Question: what are the different meanings of *after* on the above lines?
Hint: replace *after* with *following.* Where does it change the meaning or not make sense?

Comment

Following is not possible on line 6; it cannot be used as a **conjunction** and this supports the conclusion reached in Activity A. However, it also fails to work on line 2 (because *after* has a different meaning here: 'seeking'), and on line 3 because there is a strong relationship with the preceding word *looking*. *Look after* is an idiomatic expression (meaning 'take care of') called a **prepositional verb** (see Chapter 9).

Activity C

Technique 3: add some little words.
Question: what forms of the verb *set* are shown on the lines below? *Set* is a very irregular verb; the form 'set' can represent the infinitive, present tense, past tense and **-ed** participle.
Hint: see if the lines can be expanded by placing *which* or *it* and a form of the verb *be* in front of *set.*

1. The firm said... the bionauts **set** a new world record...
2. ... something which if **set** in a contemporary context...
3. From a crest above the hut we watched the sun **set** on a line of peaks...
4. The science-fiction thriller topped the record **set** nearly a year ago...

Comment

On lines 1 and 3 nothing can be done as *set* represents the **past tense**. (If it was the **present tense**, the form would be *sets*.)

On lines 2 (*...if it is set...*) and 4 (*...which was set...*) expansion is possible. This shows that *set* is an **-ed participle** and that the sentence is **passive** in meaning. It also indicates that the verb *set* is **transitive** (see Chapter 7).

Activity D

Technique 4: try moving words around
Question: what is the relationship between *turn* and the word following it?
Hint: on this line decide whether the short word following the three examples of *turn* can be moved elsewhere.

Turn down the heating when not required. Use natural light whenever possible. **Turn off** unwanted lights. **Turn off** machinery when not in use.

Comment

In each case the word can be moved:
  Turn the heating **down** when not required. **Turn** unwanted lights **off**. **Turn** machinery **off** when not in use.

  This is sufficient to identify *turn down* and *turn on* as a particular type of verb: as **phrasal verbs**. (See Chapter 9 for more on this, in particular for cases where movement is not possible.)

Activity E

Technique 5: change the form of the keyword
Question: What is the meaning of *memory* on these lines? With **nouns** that can be both **count** and **noncount** but with different meanings (see Chapter 1), one way to identify the meaning is to turn a **singular** form into a **plural** (and make any other changes if necessary, e.g. changing the **verb** form). *Memory* has two distinct meanings. In one it refers to the human faculty for remembering things; in the other it refers to the actual things we remember.
Hint: try to turn *memory* into the plural without changing the meaning.

1. It causes them to suffer temporary lapses of **memory**...
2. ...the Atari VCS is just a fond **memory**.
3. In her **memory** the classes contributed towards the purchase of class equipment...
4. You all gave us a day to remember and a **memory** we'll never forget.
5. Has it ever been, in your **memory**, postponed or cancelled...?
6. It seemed pretty arty but some scenes stick in the **memory**.

Comment

Pluralising *memory* only makes sense on lines 2 (*they are just fond memories*) and 4 (*memories we'll never forget*). The presence of *a* on both lines is another useful clue (see Technique 1).

Activity F

Technique 6: work out the meaning and relate this to the grammar.
Question: what kind of noun is *customs* on these lines? *Customs* has two distinct grammatical possibilities. In one it is the **plural** of *custom*, meaning a 'habit' or 'tradition'. In the other it is a noun that only occurs in the plural; it refers to the control we go through when entering a country. (See Chapter 1 for more on this.)
Hint: Use the context of the keyword to help you guess the meaning of *customs* on the lines below, e.g. 'go through customs'.

1. ...most of its laws and many of its **customs** are about social harmony.
2. ...we use that information when we go through various **customs** and border points.
3. ...this revenue from **customs** duties and agricultural levies was hardly buoyant.
4. ...why do we have to go through **customs** anyway?
5. His knowledge encompassed...the Norman Conquest and Chinese marriage **customs**...
6. ...different actors are used to reflect local culture and **customs**.
7. ...these are likely to include increased **customs** controls...
8. Chris Luby by day is a **customs** and excise inspector...
9. ...humour may depend deeply on cultural knowledge...**customs**, music, literature, and so on.
10. I was also in agony and consequently limped out of **customs** to greet my mum.

Comment

On lines 1, 5, 6 and 9 it is the **plural** of *custom*. On lines 2, 3, 4, 7, 8 and 10 it is the non-singular **noun** *customs*.

Activity G

Technique 7: do not be distracted by unknown words
Question: What is the grammar of this sentence? Look again at this sentence from Activity F about the word *customs*. There are several words that you are perhaps unfamiliar with, underlined below:

> ...this <u>revenue</u> from **customs** <u>duties</u> and <u>agricultural</u> <u>levies</u> was hardly <u>buoyant</u>.

But the grammar is not hard to work out. You can tell that *revenue* is a **noun** because it is preceded by *this*, and that *customs duties* and *agricultural levies* are **noun phrases** because of the **plurals** and because they are joined by *and*; so *customs* here 'goes with' *duties*. The grammar of this sentence is a long **subject** (*this revenue from customs duties and agricultural levies*) followed by a form of the verb *be* and an **adjective** phrase (*hardly buoyant*). You may also need to check the meaning of *revenue* ('income') and *duty* (here a kind of tax) to work out that the sentence is about money and therefore *customs* here has the non-singular meaning.

Further work with concordance lines

If you find the activities in this book useful in your study of English grammar, it is possible to find and work on concordance lines on your own.

Most corpora are unfortunately not public; they have been built up by, and are the property of, publishers who use them to inform the dictionaries and grammars that they publish. Nowadays such corpora extend to more than a billion words. Other smaller corpora are part of research projects and equally are not accessible.

One exception to this is the British National Corpus (BNC), which was designed to be a national resource, and to which access can be purchased. It is the source of the concordance lines in this book. It is composed of texts totalling over 100 million words from all genres of English, in particular spoken as well as written. Another resource that is commercially available is Collins Cobuild Wordbanks Online, which is composed of 57 million words. It is part of the larger Bank of English (650 million words).

The best freely accessible source of concordance lines is the Corpus of Contemporary American English (COCA), which consists of 450 million words. It has a very simple user interface and can be found at corpus.byu.edu/coca/.

COCA, the BNC and other corpora mentioned above are 'generalised' corpora, which means they aim to include examples of 'everything'. Many other corpora are 'specialised', in that they focus on one particular type or genre of English, usually with a research purpose in mind. If you are interested in a particular type of English (e.g. business communication) it is possible to make your own corpus.

Of course, corpora are not only used for extracting concordance lines. One other common exploitation, to which an occasional reference is made in the chapters below, is frequency lists: which words are most common in texts. Other more refined analyses are possible, for example to do with collocation: whether words go together with one another more often than one would statistically expect. In this way more than just the grammar of English can be studied.

Chapter 1

Nouns

1.0 Introduction

Nouns are the most numerous **word class** in English, but individually they tend not to be as frequent as the grammatical (or 'function') word classes, such as **prepositions** and **determiners**. The most common nouns, *time* and *people*, are the 76th and 80th most frequent words in English, according to one frequency list (and that is without discounting their occasional use as verbs). Nouns have a number of interesting features which are not dealt with here: the distinction between **singular** and **plural** (sometimes formed irregularly), the (Saxon) **genitive** and their formation with certain derivational endings (such as *-tion* or *-ment*).

A number of important factors are focussed on in the activities below. By far the most important is whether the noun is **'count'** or **'noncount'**. Thus, certain nouns can be 'counted' grammatically in the sense that they can be preceded by *a/an* or *one*, *two* or any other numeral. A typical count noun would be *car*: *a car*, *two cars*. Noncount nouns cannot be 'counted'. For example, *advice*: you cannot say **an advice* or **two advices* (though you can use a counting expression: *two pieces of advice*; here *piece* is the count noun).

Many nouns can be both count and noncount, often with little change in meaning (other than referring to a mass of something or an individual item), e.g. *string/a string, divorce/a divorce*. In other cases we regard one form as the basic and the other as derived from it by a process of **'conversion'**, with a predictable difference in meaning. Thus, *a dog* (count) can become *dog* (noncount) to refer to the meat. This process is systematic since it applies to other animals and their meat.

However, in many cases the difference between the count and noncount meanings, though there is a relationship, is neither predictable nor systematic. A good example is *room*. As a count noun it refers to a unit of a building; as a noncount noun it means 'space'. They could almost be treated as different lexical items.

The choice of determiners is also influenced by the count status of a noun. Thus, *much* is restricted to noncount nouns and *many* to count (plural) nouns. *Little* and *few* are similarly constrained. *The*, unlike *a/an*, can be used with both types of noun, however, as can *this* and *that*. *Some* is usually used with noncount nouns to refer to a vague quantity (*some money*) and count nouns in the plural to refer to a vague number (*some people*), but it can also be used with count singular nouns to indicate something or someone unknown:

> *Some student was looking for you.*

Another feature of nouns is that some only occur in the plural form. *Trousers* and *binoculars* are good examples; we cannot say **a trouser/binocular*. These are sometimes called plural nouns. However, in many such cases, there is a singular form but with a very different meaning, which may in turn have its own plural. Thus *arms* can either be a distinct plural noun meaning 'weapons', or the plural of *arm*, meaning 'limbs'.

This factor may combine with the count status of a noun. Thus, *glass* can either be a noncount noun referring to the substance, or a count noun referring to the item we drink from. (The relationship is not predictable because *a glass* does not refer to anything made of glass, such as a window; indeed, a 'glass' may be made of plastic.) However, *glasses* can either be the plural of *a glass* or a distinct plural noun meaning 'spectacles'.

A third factor focussed on below is the sub-class of '**collective nouns**'. Certain singular count nouns can take a plural verb form (if they are the subject) when they are regarded as referring to a group of individuals. For example:

> The <u>government</u> <u>have</u> decided…

The alternative with a singular verb form is possible, if the speaker/writer wishes to convey the idea a single body:

> The <u>government</u> <u>has</u> decided…

With such nouns a plural form is possible of course: *The <u>governments</u> have agreed…*

A final feature of nouns, very different from the different sub-classes identified above, is their function in **noun phrases**. Nouns are typically thought of as the **head** of noun phrases; for example, *a profitable <u>business</u>*. But very often they function as a **premodifier**, in front of a head noun: *a <u>business</u> student*. In this case the distinction between count and noncount will not be formally marked by an accompanying determiner, for example; however, the meaning is usually the noncount one. This will be relevant in some of the exercises below.

The nouns selected below are not necessarily the most frequent, but they are representative of the important factors outlined above.

1.1 wood

As explained above in 1.0, many nouns can be both count and noncount with a difference in meaning. Sometimes this difference is predictable, but sometimes it is not; in these cases the count and noncount versions of such words seem to refer to separate lexical ideas. This is certainly the case with *wood*. As a count noun it refers to a collection of trees, smaller than a forest; for example:

> We camped in a small <u>wood</u> at the side of the road.

As a noncount noun it means the material obtained from trees used for building, for making fires, etc.:

> Different types of wood burn differently.

Activity 1.1

Look at these lines and decide whether *wood* is a:

a. count noun
b. noncount noun.

Hints:

- Look at the determiner used with *wood*. If there is no determiner, it is noncount (assuming of course that it is the head of the noun phrase); if there is *a*, then it is count.
- Work out the meaning; if *wood* refers to the material then it is noncount, if it is a place consisting of trees then count.

1. …it's finished in an attractive shade that enhances the natural grain of the **wood**.
2. [It] consisted of rough grazing, perhaps within a **wood**.
3. So, I used the ship's sails, rope, and pieces of **wood**, and after a lot of hard work I had a very fine tent.
4. …he's imagining the fox walking through the **wood** and coming towards his window.
5. Our house is made of **wood** and is dark green.
6. Only wych elm grew in the **wood** and it burned for me quite well when dry.
7. And is it not the best **wood** for coffins?
8. Many town-dwellers burn **wood** for pleasure.
9. Once one gets the taste for smoking **wood** it is possible to mix and obtain subtle flavours…
10. Regular visitors include two **wood** pigeons, seven collar doves, innumerable rooks and jackdaws.

1.2 promise

Promise is another of the nouns discussed in 1.0 that are both count and noncount, but where the two meanings are quite different. As a count noun it means something that you say as a guarantee of future action:

He's broken his promise again.

whereas as a noncount noun it means 'potential':

She has lots of promise.

The adjective *promising* is related to this meaning, whereas the verb *promise* usually refers to the count meaning.

Activity 1.2

Look at the lines below and decide whether *promise* is a:

a. count noun
b. noncount noun.

(*Note*: over half the occurrences of *promise* are the verb; these are not included.)

Hint: try to pluralise *promise* (making other necessary changes). If this is possible without changing the meaning then it is a count noun.

1. ...progress on the trunk road is now a firm **promise**...
2. She is already a lacemaker of great **promise**...
3. This new venture seems to hold great **promise** for the future...
4. And, in the end, if much of the **promise** is still unfulfilled, in his own words, 'I ain't done too bad'.
5. She recalled a **promise** made by Mr Major when he became Prime Minister...
6. ...an environment unnaturally charged with emotion and hooked on an expensive **promise** of love and everlasting life.
7. The Society also gained some interesting new facts regarding the BCR, together with the **promise** of some more photographic material.
8. Notwithstanding this **promise**, the use of road pricing to change travel habits still seems some way off.
9. But Mr Clarke's statements since the meeting give the impression that he reneged on his **promise** to us.
10. ...[they] died young, their **promise** unfulfilled, like everyone from Jimmy Blanton to Charlie Parker.

1.3 *business*

Business is another noun that changes meaning according to whether it is count or noncount, without a predictable relationship between the two meanings. As a count noun it indicates a company or a particular activity; as a noncount noun, it refers to trade and commercial activity, or activity in general.

> He's been running his own *business* since he was 17. (count)
> This outbreak is a terrible *business*. (count)
> I've got no head for *business*. (noncount)

It is commonly used as a premodifier in a noun phrase:

> We offer a comprehensive range of services for the *business traveller*.

Activity 1.3

Work out on these lines whether *business* is a:

a. count noun
b. noncount noun. (There is also one line where it is a **premodifier**.)

Hint: try to pluralise *business* (making other necessary changes). If this is possible without changing the meaning then it is a count noun.

1. Scotch Whisky is a core **business** for all of them.
2. Winning The Queen's Awards brings prestige, credibility and increased **business**.
3. [It] has been an international **business** for over 230 years.
4. The safest way to ensure that you are getting the best practical **business** advice for your money is...
5. And multi-player games are good for **business**.

6. ...all the important legal developments likely to affect your **business**...
7. ...[he] reckons that **business** is now becoming so complex that he needs a new core of trained administrators.
8. His romantic northern-sounding address...helped his **business** more than a little.
9. ...MPs are now thrashing through the **business** of submitting themselves to their local parties.
10. This is forcing people to equip themselves with computers in a hurry. This is not an easy **business**.

1.4 work

Work is another noun which can be both count and noncount, with largely unrelated meanings. As a noncount noun it refers to formal activity or employment:

> *I've got <u>work</u> to do.*
> *What time do you finish <u>work</u> today?*

(In this meaning one equivalent count noun is *job*.) It can also be the place where people are employed:

> *She's not at <u>work</u> today.*

When it is count it generally refers to a work of art. It is also common as a verb.

Activity 1.4

Work out on these lines whether *work* is a:

a. count noun
b. noncount noun. (There is also one line where it is a **premodifier**.)

Hint: sometimes a verb can indicate the count status of a following noun. You do or carry out *work*, but you create *a work*.

1. It also fits in with **work** being carried out at other research centres.
2. ...a biblical text was used to create another well-known **work** by the son...
3. Since we offer training as part of our technical support contract, this **work** can easily be done by any office worker.
4. All participants are **work** colleagues.
5. Without their efforts this vital **work** could not be done.
6. In this second edition the standard **work** has been fully revised with a number of new photographs.
7. In return she will do research or voluntary **work**.
8. If the outdoor **work** is not for you, there are many ways in which you can still help.
9. [The artists] are also displaying some of their **work**.
10. The Trust's annual cycle rides have always proved popular and successful in raising funds for our **work**.

1.5 *play*

As a count noun *play* usually refers to the works of a playwright: *the plays of Shakespeare* (and for which the closest noncount equivalent is *drama*). As a noncount noun it refers to sporting or entertaining activity (*Play is good for children*), where it is closely related in meaning to the verb *play*.

Activity 1.5

Work out whether *play* on these lines is:

a. count
b. noncount.

Hint: work out the meaning.

1. I am reminded of a line in Tony Kushner's **play** Angels in America...
2. But this emphasis is rather distorting for the **play** as a whole...
3. The six championship courts (five glass-backed) provide ideal conditions for **play**...
4. Henry V offers, better than any other **play** in the repertoire, what might be called a yuppie dynamic...
5. Science lends itself to learning through **play**.
6. Each **play** is treated separately in its own section and no comparison among them is made.
7. ...we are simply presented with certain aspects of the **play**'s style and development.
8. Cancellations notified to Reception before the day of **play** will not be charged.

1.6 *space*

As a count noun *space* refers to a specific empty area:

> *I couldn't find a parking* <u>*space*</u>.

In this it is related in meaning to the noncount use, referring to a non-specific area:

> *It's a waste of* <u>*space*</u>.

However, there is another unrelated noncount meaning where it refers to the universe outside the planet Earth:

> <u>*Space*</u>: *the final frontier*...

Activity 1.6

Decide whether *space* on the following lines is a:

a. count noun
b. noncount noun referring to the universe
c. noncount noun referring to an indefinite empty area.

Hint: try to pluralise *space* without changing the meaning (making other necessary changes).

1. Blooms of certain species of coccolithophores are so vast that they can be seen from **space**…
2. When the sun's rays hit the Earth a lot of the heat is reflected back into **space**…
3. Unfortunately, limits of **space** dictate that I cannot discuss all of the essays in the book…
4. …these videos are indispensable to anyone interested in **space** exploration.
5. There is no **space** here to examine this issue in detail…
6. The need for more **space** led to the move to the present offices…
7. Turn back to the beginning, and print the child's name in the **space** on the title page…
8. Please make sure that you write down your registration number in the **space** provided on the sponsor form.
9. Home-made compost is wonderful, but you will need a lot of **space** to make the necessary amount.
10. In fact, we know that if we get into a confined **space** with the intention of defying gravity we are running a risk…

1.7 room

Room as a noncount noun is similar in meaning to 'space', whereas as a count noun it refers to a unit of a building. These two uses can be demonstrated in one example:

There's no <u>room</u> in that <u>room</u>.

The first instance is noncount, the second count.

Activity 1.7

In these lines identify one line where *room* is noncount and another where it appears to be noncount but in fact is count.

Hint: try to pluralise *room*.

1. Deep down in a blue half light of the control **room**, sailors huddle over their radar screens…
2. That man's recorded everything that was said in this **room**.
3. …I haven't put that on, because I haven't got **room**.
4. Strangely, though, the symptoms returned to me every night when I retired to my bunk which occupied a corner of the same **room**.
5. If there was the slightest breeze from any direction the smoke would spread itself evenly between chimney and **room** in more or less equal proportions…
6. It is in the blending **room** that the mature Scotch Whiskies are combined with each other…
7. How can Anna get Carl from the window of the **room** to the fire escape?
8. …theirs was the **room** with the broken bolt hanging from the door…

1.8 *arms*

The form 'arms' can either be a plural noun (see 1.0) meaning 'weapons', for example:

> *The treaty specifies a reduction in conventional <u>arms</u>.*

or the plural of a count noun referring to the part of the body:

> *She put her <u>arms</u> around me.*

It is not possible to say *an arm* meaning 'a weapon'; this could only refer to the body part. In the plural meaning, *arms* is often a premodifier: *the <u>arms</u> <u>race</u>*.

Activity 1.8

Identify the lines below where *arms* is a plural noun. In which is it a premodifier?

Hint: try replacing *arms* with *weapons*.

1. But they also throw up their **arms**, and say there is nothing they can do except hope that people power will prevail...
2. Then press upwards until the **arms** are locked straight out...
3. The help will come in the form of technology originally developed in the USA for the **arms** industry...
4. They lay in each other's **arms**...
5. ...the **arms** trade brings income at a time of serious recession...
6. If you aren't using flags, cross your **arms** in front of your body...
7. I held out my hands to my father as he came into the room, and he took me in his **arms**.
8. If you wanted to make a person at a distance come over to you you'd probably wave your **arms**.
9. They're like the **arms** of the same monster.
10. [It] has been variously described in the technical press as designed to monitor Soviet compliance with **arms** treaties...

1.9 *customs*

Customs, like *arms*, can either be a plural noun referring to the organisation that controls the passage of goods into a country (when it is often capitalised), or the plural of a count noun, meaning 'habits' or 'traditions'. As the former it is often a premodifier.

Activity 1.9

Identify in the lines below where *customs* is a count noun in the plural. Say also whether it is a premodifier.

Hint: look at the words that follow *customs*.

1. Thereafter he spoke on two occasions (1723 and 1725) on **customs** matters...
2. The future of the industry also depends on ease of access to the ports and a smooth progression through **customs** and immigration procedures.

3. The growth of industrialisation...resulted in the collapse of the old traditionally supported **customs** and public charities.
4. We were required to get four stamps on a form, German **customs** and passport control...
5. All **customs** barriers will be removed from trade in some 20,000 species...
6. It...ensures the preservation and display of the objects, **customs** and beliefs of our past.
7. On the way, we stopped at the border and went through the immigration and **customs** formalities...
8. The problem is that you are dealing with foreigners who insist on having different money, **customs**, languages, politics, legislation and living a long way away.
9. Wildlife control operations are being co-ordinated with the army, police and **customs**...
10. Compatability: does the product fit with the **customs**, values and experience of the consumers?

1.10 *team*

Team is a collective noun (see 1.0). In other words, it can be considered plural to suggest a collection of individuals even though there is no -*s* ending:

The <u>team</u> <u>are</u> having a wonderful time.

To use it as a singular would suggest a single body or unit:

The <u>team</u> <u>is</u> in danger of being relegated.

This, of course, is only evident when the noun is the head of a noun phrase which is the subject of a verb form which distinguishes between singular and plural subjects. In most cases the distinction will not be obvious, either because the noun is not the subject or because the verb form does not distinguish singular and plural.

It is, of course, also possible to have a plural of the noun:

We'll play against four <u>teams</u>.

Activity 1.10

Decide whether *team* on the lines below is being used with:

a. singular verb agreement
b. plural verb agreement, or
c. whether it is impossible to be certain.

Hint: where possible, try replacing the subject noun phrase with *it* or *they*.

1. The offshore **team** are nearing completion of their operations manual...
2. The same **team** are doing some friends of ours on Main Road...
3. [He] said his **team** had found a way of predicting the migration patterns of harmful aphids...
4. This year the new editorial **team** has made great strides to develop the editorial content within a limited budget.

5. The **team**, led by sub-officer Harry Dawson, aim to ride in 25 mile stages and reach Dublin within eight hours.
6. Analysis of the gas in the balloon told the **team** how much oxygen the camels were using as they walked.
7. The first project to reach a conclusion was the **team** looking at the interface between our personnel and wages departments.
8. Penny has a wealth of catering industry experience in both operations and sales and the **team** is reaping the benefits of her expertise.
9. The radio **team** say their aim is to 'establish ourselves as true social communicators'…
10. The same **team** followed that up just ten days later with a French day to commemorate the storming of the Bastille on July 14.

1.11 *committee*

Like *team*, *committee* is a collective noun which, if a subject, may appear with a plural verb form if it is considered to refer to a collection of individuals rather than a single body: *the committee <u>has</u>/<u>have</u> decided…*

Activity 1.11

In all of the lines below *committee* is the subject of the following verb. In which cases:

a. does it represent a single body?
b. does it represent a collection of individuals?
c. is it not clear, because the verb form is not marked for singular or plural?

Hint: Try replacing *committee* with *it* or *they* according to the following verb.

1. [These] have to be met from donations, raffles, sales etc., organised by a **committee** who are interested in animal welfare.
2. The planning **committee** decided on Monday evening to defer its decision about the application until after that meeting.
3. A Cabinet **committee**, expected to be chaired by the Prime Minister, will be set up soon…
4. …the executive **committee** have agreed to changes in the way that the organisation works with its members on policy issues…
5. The World Environment Day Honor **Committee** includes U.N. Secretary General Javier Perez de Cuellar…
6. Your **Committee** has held meetings on 3 April, 22 May and 19 June 1989.
7. But the Nobel Prize **committee** said the prize was not a declaration of sainthood.
8. He added that the **committee** was concerned about the lack of car parking spaces on the proposed site
9. …she is already busy in her new role, well supported by the Executive **Committee** which now has four new members…
10. The **committee** will therefore include ministers from most of the main Whitehall departments.

Chapter 2

Personal pronouns

2.0 Introduction

The so-called **personal pronouns** are some of the most frequent words in English and on the surface seem to be quite straightforward to use. However, they have some unexpected uses which often do not correspond to the way the supposed equivalents in other languages are used. They also exhibit some grammatical categories (gender and case) which are not found elsewhere in English.

The normal way of summing up the personal pronouns is by means of a table which shows the relationships between the different forms: the so-called 'personal pronoun paradigm'. This involves a number of factors, namely **person** (first, second or third), **number** (singular or plural), **case** (subjective or objective) and **gender** (masculine, feminine or neuter). Not all of these distinctions operate for every word, as Table 2.1 shows (for example, singular and plural are not distinguished for *you*).

The table captures the formal relationships between the words, but it does not show how they are used. In particular, it misses a crucial distinction between **specific reference** and **generic reference**. *We*, *you* and *they* can all have generic reference; that is, they can all refer to people in general, as well as to specific groups that are known to both speaker and hearer. Their generic uses are explained below in the relevant sections.

The words selected below are mainly the **subjective** pronouns, e.g. *we* and *they*, but the related forms – **objective** (*us*, *them*, etc.), **possessive determiner** (e.g. *our* and *their*) and **possessive pronoun** (*ours*, *theirs*, etc.) (sometimes collectively called the 'central pronouns') – follow the same pattern of usage. In order to give more widespread coverage, two words which are not the subjective forms are included: *her* (an objective form, as well as possessive determiner) and *myself* (a **reflexive pronoun**).

Generally the words selected here only function as pronouns, but *her*, *you* and *we* are also used as **determiners** (but different types). Other words which are used as pronouns (but not

Table 2.1 The personal pronoun paradigm

	First	Second	Third		
			Masculine	Feminine	Neuter
Singular	I/me	you	he/him	she/her	it
Plural	we/us	you	they/them		

(Where there are two forms inside a box, separated by a slash, these represent the subjective and objective forms)

personal pronouns) are included in Chapter 3. A further word, *one*, which is also used as a personal pronoun, is covered in Chapter 12.

2.1 *you*

You seems to be a very straightforward word: it is the 'second person' pronoun, referring to the listener(s) or reader(s) in the act of communication:

> *How are you feeling?*
> *You may not leave the room until the exam is over.*

The only obvious irregularities about it are that, unlike the other personal pronouns, it does not distinguish between singular and plural reference (cf. *I* and *we*), or between the subjective and objective (cf. *I* and *me*). In the latter case, its position in the sentence helps to disambiguate (*You like me* vs *I like you*), while in the former the context usually makes it clear whether one person or more than one is intended (and if it does not, the ambiguity may be intentional).

In English, as well as referring to a specific individual or individuals who are being addressed by the speaker/writer, *you* is quite commonly used to refer 'generically' – that is, to make a generalisation – more so than its equivalents in other languages.

> *It's awful when you can't remember someone's name.*
> *You add the eggs to the butter, not the other way round.*

In these examples *you* is not addressing anyone in particular.

> *You* can also be used as a determiner in front of a noun to get people's attention:

> *You boys line up over there.*

One particular combination of this, *you guys*, is nowadays used in British English, as well as American, as an informal plural personal pronoun (with *you* reserved for singular reference):

> *I don't know about you guys, but I've had enough.*

This can refer to women as well as men.

Activity 2.1

On the following lines firstly identify whether *you* is a:

a. pronoun being used to make a generalisation
b. pronoun referring to specific readers or listeners
c. determiner.

Hint: try replacing *you* with *one*.

1. As a member of a local group **you** can receive a newsletter and attend regular social meetings.
2. We are now facing the most serious challenge in our history and depend on **you** for support.
3. And because we know how expensive a new baby can be, **you** can choose all **you** need now and spread the cost with our 16 weeks FREE CREDIT.

4. I recommend **you** to contact the trust for information...
5. I've got a message for **you** as well.
6. What's the matter with **you** people, don't **you** listen to the patients any more?
7. Dogs and sheep have died after drinking near blooms, where the toxins tend to concentrate. But **you** don't have to swallow the water to become ill.
8. At the end of the tenancy **you** will be required to refix the fence on the original boundary.
9. The more the government does, the less **you**'re free to do.
10. I...write to confirm the terms on which we would be prepared to licence **you** to occupy the area of garden land adjacent to your property.

2.2 we

We is usually introduced as the plural first-person personal pronoun, the singular being I. But we is not the 'plural' of I, except in very rare cases where two people say the same thing simultaneously, or when several people sign the same letter ('We, the undersigned...'). Otherwise we is usually a combination of the speaker plus the second person (I + you) or the speaker plus the third person (I + he/she/they). The first case is called 'inclusive we', because it includes the hearers, while the second is called 'exclusive we' because it excludes the hearers, for example:

> What shall we do tonight? (inclusive)
> Where did you spend your holidays? – We went to the seaside. (exclusive)

Often it is not clear whether reference is inclusive or exclusive, as in this example from a book on English grammar:

> In speech we can give words extra stress...

It is not clear if the writer is including readers (teachers or learners of English) in this action.

Sometimes the inclusive use extends to all persons, i.e. to include everybody in a certain community, whether they are listening or not; we may call this 'all-inclusive':

> We must all be prepared to make sacrifices. (said by a politician)

Sometimes we can refer back to an earlier noun phrase, just like the third-person pronouns he, she, it and they:

> Hong Kong has been lucky that in the past...we did and we still do enjoy a high level of press freedom.

We, like you, can also be used as a determiner in front of a noun:

> We students never have any power.

Activity 2.2

Work out whether we on the lines below is

a. exclusive
b. inclusive.

Say what evidence there is; it may not always be clear. In two exclusive cases it is referring back to a particular noun phrase.

Hint: look for some contrast with *you*.

1. **We** also hope you will follow our campaigns in your quarterly newsletter...
2. The National Council for Civil Liberties is a non-partisan, voluntary organisation... **We** are now facing the most serious challenge in our history and depend on you for support.
3. **We** deliver right to your door FREE of charge.
4. Right, well, welcome to Atlantic two five two. Today **we**'ll be meeting Dannii Minogue.
5. The Trust's annual cycle rides have always proved popular and successful in raising funds for our work. This year's is the biggest ever and **we**'re asking everyone who cares about wildlife to sponsor the cyclists or make a donation.
6. ...and supporting our work to safeguard the future of biological and medical research. Unless **we** work together to counter this threat, the contribution to knowledge, medicine and health that will come from research will be in jeopardy.
7. **We** held a meeting about this on Thursday and Friday.
8. Unlike many other publishers...**we** publish all our own books.
9. However, if on checking the estimate with the reading on your meter you find your consumption is very different from the estimate **we** shall willingly amend the bill to your own reading.
10. Over the last ten years, the Government has removed many of the freedoms **we** take for granted.

2.3 *they*

Traditionally, *they* is described as the third-person plural personal pronoun, typically being used to refer back to a definite group of things or people:

> There was a group of <u>people</u> standing around something on the ground. I could see <u>they</u> were quite upset.
> <u>Her paintings</u> were lying on the ground; <u>they</u> were all torn and dirty.

It represents the subject of the clause.

However, very often *they* is not referring back to something already mentioned but rather to some unspecified group from which the speaker feels distant – the government, experts, etc.:

> It doesn't matter what you do, <u>they</u>'ll still get you.
> <u>They</u> say income tax is going to go up.

Another way in which *they* differs from its traditional role is in its use to refer back to a singular, indefinite human where the gender is unclear and where to use *he* or *she* would therefore be inappropriate, for example:

> Someone's been talking, haven't <u>they</u>?

This use is somewhat controversial, but it is quite common, has been a feature of English for a long time, and avoids other clumsy or sexist constructions, such as *he, he and she*, or *s/he*. (Try putting these in the above example.)

Activity 2.3

Work out what *they* refers to on the following lines. In most cases it is referring back to a plural noun earlier in the text but in one case it is referring to a singular referent, and in another it is referring outside the text to an unspecified group of authorities.

The lines are longer than usual in order to show the possible referents.

Hint: Check whether it would be feasible to replace *they* with *he or she*.

1. The Government has recently accepted a recommendation … for a doubling in the number of trained consultants…but it will take 10 years before **they** are all in place.
2. In the tropical oceans reef building corals have been responding to climatic changes for hundreds of years. **They** act as living tape recorders of the past.
3. … there's a lot of cast iron and steel in our engine and marine engines don't like that, **they** prefer brass.
4. Popes lack the machinery to administer crackdowns. **They** can only issue briefs, bulls, encyclicals and the occasional definition.
5. It is very difficult to get essential oil from the rose, it has to be done by what **they** call extraction. **They** put it on a solvent or a fat in layers and let the oil seep through…
6. Nobody was forcing the defendants to do what **they** did. **They** were not persuaded or encouraged to do what **they** did.
7. [In this situation] your casualty may literally shriek as **they** go down…
8. …Nearly all interviewees claimed **they** had been forced to cut down on food and fuel…
9. Every minister now looks at his biggest decisions in the light of how **they** will affect the general election…
10. This information is indeed worth treasuring, but it's not what most people imagine when **they** think about wrecks.

2.4 *her*

Her has two roles; as the **objective** pronoun form of *she*, representing the third-person singular feminine pronoun; for example:

> Give *her* the benefit of the doubt.

or as the equivalent **possessive determiner**:

> *Her* presence is not welcome here.

With other personal pronouns these two roles have separate words: *me/my*, *him/his*, etc.

Activity 2.4

Decide whether *her* on these lines is:

a. an objective pronoun
b. a possessive determiner

Hint: look at the position of *her*.

1. Two years ago **her** mother burned to death in a mystery fire in the same house.
2. Even a professional footballer is among **her** clients.
3. I could get a doctor to go and see **her** and phone.
4. But I don't think we should give **her** too long…
5. …is it okay for **her** to take these?
6. …there are signs that **her** crusade is gradually grinding to a halt.

2.5 *myself*

Myself is one of the 'reflexive' personal pronouns, and it has been chosen as representative of them. The reflexive pronouns, *myself, yourself, himself, herself, itself, ourselves, yourselves* and *themselves*, allow the object of the verb to refer to the same person(s) as the subjects, e.g.

> I blame <u>myself</u>.

This is particularly important with third-person pronouns, where the use of the objective forms (*him, her, it* and *them*) could only refer to others. Thus, *he hurt him* involves two people whereas *he hurt himself* involves only one. Reflexive pronouns can also be used to show identity with an object, e.g.

> We'll need to help <u>them</u> feed <u>themselves</u>.

or with a subject after a preposition:

> <u>I</u> don't know what to do <u>with</u> <u>myself</u>.

The other main use of these pronouns is to emphasise a subject, meaning that nobody else is involved, e.g.

> <u>I</u> invented it <u>myself</u>.
> <u>I</u> <u>myself</u> had a disturbing experience the other day…

In this case they are called 'emphatic' pronouns.

Reflexive pronouns are sometimes used as an alternative to the objective pronouns in certain situations; for example in lists:

> The speakers this morning are <u>myself</u>, Dan and June… (Also …are <u>me</u>, Dan…)

Activity 2.5

Decide whether *myself* in the lines below is:

a. an emphatic pronoun
b. a reflexive pronoun
c. an alternative to *me*.

Hint: try moving *myself* around the sentence.

1. I think I'll need to see about it **myself**.
2. I can hear **myself** talking all the time.
3. …I'm usually not too bad at keeping a grip on **myself**.

4. I've been looking after **myself** of course.
5. I would say I've been pretty lucky recently **myself**.
6. I can remember being a student **myself**.
7. I am sure **myself** that Europe is stronger when Britain, France and Germany are working together...
8. My thanks for the hospitality and friendliness accorded to **myself** and my comrades...
9. Well, I'm still getting **myself** in a tangle...
10. I probably made **myself** a bit of a nuisance when I came in last time...
11. I found **myself** surreptitiously studying him.
12. [Could it] be explained perhaps in rather simple language to people like **myself**?

2.6 *it*

It is one of the most frequent words in English; in one frequency list it is in eighth position. On the surface it seems to be a simple word to use and understand, but there are a number of unusual ways in which it is used, although it is always a pronoun.

It is usually described as the 'third-person singular neuter personal pronoun' ('neuter' as opposed to 'masculine' *he* and 'feminine' *she*). It is used to refer to things rather than people (which suggests that the term 'personal' pronoun is misleading):

It's an unusual word. (referring back to a particular word)
This car? I bought it ages ago.

However, *it* is much more interesting (or complicated) than this. Very often it is not referring to anything at all; these are the so-called 'dummy' uses of *it*, where it supplies a subject (since subjects are obligatory in English) in constructions where a logical subject is lacking; for example, when answering a phone (in British English):

Who's speaking? It's me.

or when talking about the weather:

It's raining.

We could not say that *it* refers to rain here (*the rain is raining!?*) or the weather (*the weather is raining!?*). Other languages express these ideas in different ways. There are also cases where it is a kind of dummy object, referring to nothing in colloquial, idiomatic expressions, such as *leg it* ('run away'), *hold it* ('stop!'), etc.:

We had no option but to leg it.

There are other situations where there is a vague reference to general circumstances; for example, health:

Why are you in pain? – It's my stomach, Doctor.

There is another situation where dummy *it* is used: in so-called 'cleft' sentences, where one item has been picked out from a sentence for special emphasis and placed after *it* and a part of the verb *be*, followed by a relative clause containing the less important information, for example:

It's the heat that I can't stand.

Here, *the heat* is emphasised. Compare this to a simple sentence:

> *I can't stand the heat.*

There is one more common situation where *it* is used. This is the so-called 'anticipatory' or 'preparatory' *it*, where *it* has taken the place as subject of a longer construction which has been placed at the end of the sentence because it would sound clumsy or unclear as a subject; for example:

> <u>It</u> *would be a good idea* <u>to hide your money</u>.
> <u>It</u> *would be nice* <u>if you could warn us next time</u>.
> <u>It</u> *is obvious* <u>that they cheated in the exam</u>.

As can be seen, *it* 'anticipates' a **non-finite clause** (*to...*) or a full **clause** (*if...*, *that...*). This is sometimes called 'extraposition'. Compare the simple word order without *it*:

> <u>To hide your money</u> *would be a good idea.*

Anticipatory *it* can also be used with objects:

> *I like* <u>it</u> <u>when you talk French to me</u>.
> *She made* <u>it</u> *clear that* <u>she wouldn't stand for any nonsense</u>.
> *I would appreciate* <u>it</u> <u>if you could be a little more considerate</u>.

Activity 2.6

a. Look at the following lines and decide first if *it* is referring back to something earlier; say what this noun phrase is.

Hint: replace *it* with *what*, asking a question. If you can answer, then it is referring back. (For instance, with line 1 you could ask *What hurts to swallow?* but this makes no sense.)

b. Work out where *it* represents an anticipatory subject or object, i.e. a case of extraposition.

Hint: try replacing *it* with a construction from the end of the sentence.

c. In the remaining cases work out whether *it* is referring to nothing or circumstances in general, or is part of an idiomatic expression.

1. Does **it** hurt to swallow?
2. ...what can I do for you today? – **It**'s my stomach again...
3. However, if too much phosphorus gets into lakes and rivers **it** can encourage excessive growth of the microscopic plant life...
4. Transcendental Meditation has never acquired the reputation of a sinister cult, but doubts are sometimes voiced about **it**.
5. *Parasitology* will still publish papers of the same high standard [...], making **it** essential reading for all those working and researching in the field.
6. The company admitted **it** had been a tough year...
7. Take my word for **it**, I've been going for 30 years since the well was a bucket in a hole in the ground...

8. The well, dug 900 years ago and fed by springs, was deepened by seven feet last summer to 34 feet, but **it** is still in danger of drying up.

9. …they condition the water to reduce scum, help to keep the water alkaline for proper cleaning and break up the dirt on fabrics to prevent **it** settling back.

10. …why vilify the harmless bat? Far from being dirty and unsavoury **it** spends as much time grooming its fur as any fastidious cat.

11. If you wish to purchase any of the above, please complete the enclosed Proceedings Order Form […] and return **it** to the Conference Department…

12. I was on the railway for thirty years, as a driver […] And erm anyway **it** was a wonderful place…

13. Of the first edition **it** was said: The book deals with the whole gamut of infectious diseases…

14. **It** was rough going for some of the exhibitors as they put a new four-wheel drive model through its paces.

15. After careful thought **it** was decided that a final dividend of 1.6p be recommended…

16. …in 1945 he was allowed by the Allies to relocate his business in Furth, where **it** was one of the first to produce FM radios…

17. It […] still suggests that if your car will run on standard unleaded petrol, **it** will run even better on Super Plus unleaded.

18. But **it** remains essential that I know their candidates' attitudes before deciding.

19. The equipment supplied consists of a scanner, screen, keyboard and processor unit. **It** will normally produce output to floppy disk…

20. If any pack fails to please you, simply return **it** within 10 days and owe nothing.

Chapter 3

Pronouns and determiners

3.0 Introduction

Pronouns and determiners are generally thought of as two distinct word classes, the basic distinction being that determiners 'go with' nouns while pronouns stand alone. However, while there are many pronouns that cannot be determiners (e.g. *something*), most determiners can also be pronouns, with no obvious difference in meaning, a fact that has led some linguists to group them together as one word class; for example:

> I like *these*. (pronoun)
> I like *these ideas*. (determiner + noun)

Several words which appear to be only determiners, such as the so-called possessive 'adjectives' (*my*, *your*, etc., which are more correctly labelled '**possessive determiners**'), can be accounted for because they have clear pronoun equivalents (namely, *mine*, *yours*, etc.). However, there are some determiners which cannot be 'spirited away' in this manner, most obviously the two articles *a/an* and *the*, but also *no* and *every* (unless we count *none* and *every one* as their pronoun equivalents).

For the purpose of this book, it is convenient to group the two word classes together, since a major issue in understanding their grammar is whether they occur with a noun or not.

Determiners and their corresponding pronouns refer to basic ideas such as:

- quantities or amounts of things or people (the **quantifiers**, such as *much*, *many*, *some*, etc.);
- possession by, or involvement with, people (*my/mine*, etc.);
- closeness or distance from the speaker (*this*, *that*, etc.).

Because of their basic, orienting nature, determiners come first in noun phrases before any adjectives (e.g. *some* *useful* ideas).

It is important to know which types of noun determiners go with, in particular whether they are count or noncount. For instance, *much* does not go with count nouns (*much friends).

As pronouns, quantifiers are often followed by *of* and a definite noun phrase:

> *Many of us* disagree.
> *Some of the answers* were predictable.

Some of the words included in this chapter also have an adverb use; for example:

> I like her <u>more</u>.

Because they basically refer to quantities, such words can easily be used to refer to the degree or extent specified by the word. Thus, more as a deteminer/pronoun means 'a greater amount/number of something' but as an adverb means 'to a greater extent'.

Other factors that affect these words are **assertiveness** (*much, many, any*) and quantifier float, also called **delayed determiners** (*all, both*). A full explanation of these terms can be found in the glossary and in the relevant sections.

These words are commonly used in expressions, for example:

> I was <u>more or less</u> deprived of my right to free speech.

In such cases it makes little sense to treat the words independently since the meaning derives from the whole phrase. More examples are given in the sections.

Some words which are principally determiners and/or pronouns are included in Chapters 11 and 12, since they belong to other word classes as well: *little, enough, no* and *that*. Personal pronouns were dealt with in Chapter 2.

3.1 *much*

Much is used to refer to a large amount of something; as a determiner it is used with noncount nouns; for example:

> There was <u>much</u> <u>laughter</u>.

It is also used as a pronoun:

> <u>Much</u> remains to be discovered.

and as an adverb, meaning 'to a large extent':

> I don't like him <u>much</u>.

As an adverb it is commonly used to emphasise the **comparative** of adjectives and adverbs:

> It's <u>much</u> <u>harder</u> than it used to be.

And it is commonly preceded by **intensifiers**:

> He missed me by <u>this</u> <u>much</u>.

Much can sound rather formal, as in the first two examples above, unless it occurs in **nonassertive** circumstances (such as negatives), as in the third example, or with intensifiers, as in the fourth example. Sometimes it sounds wrong if used assertively:

> *I like him much.

To avoid this *a lot* (*of*) can be used. Here are the first two examples and the last one recast:

> There was <u>a lot of</u> laughter.
> <u>A lot</u> remains to be discovered.
> I like him <u>a lot</u>.

Activity 3.1

a. First of all, identify whether *much* is a determiner, pronoun or adverb on the lines below.

Hint: look at which words *much* 'goes with'.

b. On which lines does *much* sound formal? Think of an alternative word that would not sound formal.
c. On which lines is there an intensifier in front of *much*? Would it sound strange or incorrect if the intensifier was removed?

1. [Their] involvement...is **much** appreciated...
2. ...the ratio of the two concentrations doesn't change very **much**.
3. Thank you very **much**, colleagues.
4. The images are fast and sharp, so it's **much** easier to see what's going on.
5. Such re-use is, of course, **much** encouraged by a building being listed...
6. But, when you look at it in that context it becomes very **much** part of your life...
7. This does not matter too **much** for the younger pupils...
8. It would be rash to conclude too **much** from this...
9. That is not true...of any other cars with this **much** performance.
10.   ...a woman's place was very **much** in the home...
11.   ...thanks to advances made in interior packaging, [it] has **much** more room...
12. Southern and eastern Scotland and **much** of Northern Ireland will start dry...
13. **Much** of that could be saved for other uses and not simply destroyed.
14. ...**much** practical work remains to be done before such a major change...
15. the reason...was because there was too **much** rain.

3.2 *many*

Many means a large number of people or things; as a determiner it is used with plural count nouns:

> The city has <u>many</u> attractions.

It can also be a pronoun:

> This has become a crucial issue for <u>many</u>.

In this case it is not necessarily referring back to any particular group; it can refer directly to people in general. This sounds very formal.

It is often used in conjunction with **intensifiers** such as *very* to modify the idea of a large number:

> We don't have <u>very many</u> alternatives.

When used with other determiners it comes last (as a **post-determiner**):

> She's been ill <u>these many</u> weeks.

In one situation it apparently precedes another determiner:

> <u>Many an</u> investor has come to regret such a decision.

However, *many a* is best treated as a compound determiner, especially because it goes with a singular noun and verb (even though the idea is plural).

Many can sometimes sound informal, like *much*, but to a lesser degree.

Activity 3.2

On the lines below identify:

a. where *many* is a pronoun or determiner;
b. where it is preceded by intensifiers (the answers may overlap with a);
c. where there are other determiners with *many*;

Hint: look at which words *many* 'goes with'.

1. ...cross fertilisation [seems] to be the order of the day for **many** a member!
2. There are too **many** club owners who think that they can play it both ways.
3. How thrilled and grateful we all were that so **many** people turned out on our behalf.
4. We felt that it was a great tribute to us and all our **many** comrades...
5. Consumption patterns are influenced by **many** factors...
6. **Many** fail to realise a GP works an average 72-hour week.
7. **Many** items were discussed including the following...
8. This is in line with the practice of **many** large research libraries...
9. ...once in the country **many** of their needs are looked after by the Agency...
10. **Many** of us saw this as an opportunity for mankind to make a small gesture...
11. Again, there are very **many** over-valued ideas about weight...
12. Now how **many** rock stations in your forty-one years did you actually serve on?
13. **Many** said it was bliss just to sit on the bales of straw and listen to the music...
14. All properties are within easy reach of **many** shops...
15. ...let's start off by finding how **many** we have.

3.3 *more*

More is used in a number of ways grammatically – not just as a determiner and pronoun – but it always has an idea of comparison, meaning a greater amount or number or degree of something. Grammatically it can be a determiner with plural count and noncount nouns:

We need <u>more jobs</u>.
Thanks for giving me <u>more work</u>.

or an adverb helping to form the **comparative** of some adjectives and adverbs:

We'll be <u>more careful</u> next time.
Can you talk <u>more quietly</u>?

There is a potential for ambiguity between these two uses when a noun phrase has *more* as well as a premodifying adjective; for example:

We need <u>more experienced teachers</u>.

Does this mean more teachers who are experienced (*more* = determiner) or teachers who are more experienced (comparative)? It could be either.

More is also used as a pronoun:

> I can't say *more* now.

and as an adverb alone, meaning 'to a greater degree or amount':

> We should get together *more*.

It also appears in a number of expressions, for example *more than*, and it is commonly premodified by *any*, *some* and *much*:

> I can't take *any more*.

Activity 3.3a

Decide whether *more* is:

a. an adverb modifying an adjective or adverb to form a comparative
b. a determiner
c. a pronoun
d. part of an expresssion
e. an adverb on its own.

Hint: try replacing *more* with *a larger number/amount of* to see if it is a determiner.

1. The problem is that **more** and **more** heat is being kept back by a blanket of gases...
2. Ina, a teacher, was **more** cautious.
3. ...much **more** complicated issues are being decided by the county courts...
4. There was general anticipation of regulations which would insist that **more** difficult wastes were burned instead of being sent to landfill.
5. When your skin becomes damaged by sunburn it loses heat and moisture **more** easily...
6. ...the muscles can work **more** efficiently.
7. ...the Chancellor does not tax spirits **more** heavily because of their intrinsic properties...
8. I feel as if I have to use my spray **more**.
9. All these activities are aimed to ensure that as **more** job opportunities become available...
10. ...it's always easier to work **more** land than it is just a small plot of land.
11. Now I'm not going to do any **more** now...
12. I suppose a job **more** or less was always secure at that time...
13. So [it] would have cut gross income by about a fifth and net income by much **more**.
14. It would be difficult to imagine a **more** unnatural site for [him] to work on.
15. The spaceship began to shake **more**.

Activity 3.3b

On line 3, what effect would changing *much* to *many* have ('many more complicated issues')?

3.4 *most*

Most is the **superlative** form of *more*, and like *more* can be used as a determiner with plural count nouns and noncount nouns to mean the greatest number or amount of something:

> *Most tutorials are taught by teaching assistants.*
> *Most pollution is caused by old vehicles.*

or as an adverb to form the superlative of adjectives or adverbs: *most beautiful(ly)*.

There is another situation where *most* premodifies an adjective: as an intensifier meaning 'very':

> *You are most kind.*

This is a formal usage.

It is also used as a pronoun:

> *Most will vote the way they always vote.*

as an independent adverb:

> *I like it most.*

and in expressions:

> *I like it most of all.*

Activity 3.4

On the lines below decide whether *most* is:

 a. part of a superlative adjective or adverb
 b. an intensifier
 c. a determiner
 d. a pronoun.

Hint: look at which words *most* 'goes with'.

1. **Most** arrived in the morning, some only minutes after the police...
2. In **most** cases that we heard there was no real problem...
3. Although there are some children who have a natural aptitude..., **most** children need help.
4. ...turn it down a degree or two until you find the temperature you are **most** comfortable with.
5. The **most** common reason for a biomusical film is opportunism...
6. ...this movie makes for far more frightening entertainment than the **most** graphic of shock horrors.
7. ...I should be **most** grateful if you could send a copy to the Library.
8. I think it is **most** likely that the Course will be completed by then...
9. When it comes to drawing, however, **most** of us...have little idea...
10. **Most** of these studios have beautiful sea views...
11. Meals are eaten communally for the **most** part...

12. The EC is its largest and **most** rapidly growing market.
13. I thank you **most** sincerely for the honour and opportunity you have given me.
14. The Clio has been one of Renault's **most** successful models ever…
15. Landfill is **most** suitable for immobile and non-soluble waste…

3.5 *some*

Some is used as a determiner with plural count nouns and noncount nouns to indicate a rather vague quantity or number of something; for example:

> They've had <u>some</u> good <u>ideas</u>. (plural count)
> I'll give it <u>some</u> <u>thought</u>. (noncount)

A noun phrase with *some* implies a quantity, whereas a noun phrase without it merely refers to the notion in general:

> They have good ideas.

It is also used:

- as a pronoun:

> Not everyone would agree; <u>some</u> would argue for a stricter approach.

- as an adverb with numbers meaning 'approximately':

> There were <u>some</u> 20 people already there.

- as a determiner with singular count nouns referring to something or someone vague or unknown:

> There's <u>some</u> man waiting for you.

- in front of time expressions to indicate a large amount:

> It'll take <u>some</u> years.

See more on the difference between *some* and *any* in Section 3.6.

Activity 3.5

Work out whether *some* on the lines below is:

a. a determiner with plural count nouns
b. a determiner with noncount nouns
c. a determiner with singular count nouns
d. a pronoun
e. an adverb.

Hint: try using *a certain amount/number (of)* to replace *some*.

1. One year after the Intifada began, **some** 49 per cent of the population favoured it.
2. …one of the trendiest fields in biology is not **some** anti-Darwinian mysticism, but an ultra-Darwinian…

3. ...it looks at the way that **some** artists of non-British origin have come to terms with modern art...
4. In **some** cases we are sympathetic to their ideals and share their concerns.
5. Nevertheless, to **some** extent the wars reflect the breakdown of the Vienna settlement.
6. **Some** felt relief at no longer having to 'fit the job'...
7. This at least showed **some** foresight...
8. I attempted to establish the criteria according to which **some** languages were listed under their language families.
9. I need **some** money.
10. Note: **some** of the boxes on the form will be blank.
11. **Some** people say they're so convenient they forget these as well.
12. ...there's been **some** scepticism about the symbolism of weddings...
13. East Anglia: rather cloudy, mainly dry, **some** sunny intervals...
14. And this had gone on for **some** time...
15. I'll leave **some** tissues around...

3.6 *any*

Any is a difficult word to explain, partly because it does not have equivalents in other languages. It is often said that *any* is the **negative** and **interrogative** equivalent of *some*, but while this may apply in some situations, it is not completely true. The basic difference between the two words is that *some* is **assertive** while *any* is not. In other words, *some* 'asserts' the existence of something while *any* does not. This is why *any* tends to occur in negatives and interrogatives (questions); for example:

> *I haven't read <u>any</u> of his novels.*
> *Haven't you got <u>any</u> change for the taxi?*

On these lines *any* could be replaced by *none* or *no*:

> *I have read <u>none</u> of his novels.*
> *Have you got <u>no</u> change for the taxi?*

But this is not the whole picture, for *any* also occurs in other situations where something is not being asserted, such as conditions:

> *<u>If</u> there's <u>any</u> trouble, let me know.*

or sentences with a negative idea, with a word like *seldom*:

> *I've <u>seldom</u> seen <u>any</u> performance as inspiring.*

On the other hand, *some* also appears in interrogatives:

> *Would you like <u>some</u> cake?*

where the implication is that there is some cake and the expected answer is 'yes'. (It would be a strange offer to say *Would you like any cake?*) *Some* can even occur in negatives, to emphasise an opposition:

> *I didn't eat <u>some</u> of the cake; I ate <u>all</u> of it.*

Equally, *any* is found in positive situations where it has the idea of 'no matter what/which', implying that something may not occur:

Any damage will be charged to the occupant's account.

Where there is a singular count noun, *any* is close in meaning to *every*:

She has the greatest potential of any *golfer I've seen.*

Beyond this distinction, *any* has a wide range of possibilities as a determiner with:

- singular count nouns (*any problem*)
- plural count nouns (*any problems*)
- noncount nouns (*any trouble*)
- as a pronoun:

You may have seen one but I haven't seen any.

- or as an adverb, particularly before **comparatives**:

It doesn't get any better.

Activity 3.6

a. First of all, decide whether *any* is being used in non-assertive circumstances.

Hint: try replacing a negative plus *any* with *no* or *none*.

b. Second, decide if it is a determiner, pronoun or adverb. If it is a determiner, decide what kind of noun it goes with.

Note: the answers for a and b overlap.

1. But they do not grow **any** sweeter and simply begin to rot.
2. This material is protected by international copyright laws and may not be copied or redistributed in **any** way.
3. ...there will be no discussion of **any** problem.
4. Leeds has grown...probably more than **any** other city outside London.
5. ...we were not aware of the strength of local feeling against **any** development on this site.
6. I still haven't had **any** dream.
7. The standard of the buildings and gardens...is much superior to **any** other Indian campus that I saw.
8. I do not call you servants **any** longer...
9. ...it would be misleading to suggest that nobody had taken **any** notice of the Education Reform Act.
10. Are there **any** other stories that you know about Stronsay?
11. Have you had **any** problems with this one over the years?
12. ...[it] has the largest sales team of **any** British spirits company.
13. I don't have **any** problem with giving people financial incentive...
14. **Any** help would be welcome.
15. No, they haven't changed **any** at all.

3.7 *less*

Less is used for making negative comparisons; it is a sort of negative equivalent of *more*, in that it is used with nouns to refer to a smaller amount of something; for example:

There'll be <u>less demand</u> for coal this winter.

and with adjective and adverbs to form negative comparatives:

It was <u>less interesting</u> than I expected.

However, while *more* is used quite freely with both count plural nouns (*more friends*) and noncount nouns (*more money*), there is some controversy about whether *less* should be used with the former: *less friends?* The argument is that *fewer* is 'correct' with plural count nouns: *fewer friends*. An examination of usage shows that *less* is quite common with such nouns, and, in fact, always has been. The injunction to use *fewer* dates from the late eighteenth century, until when *less* had been quite uncontroversial, and it still is when followed by *than*:

<u>*Less than*</u> *10 people a year are affected by this disease.*

It is also used as an adverb alone:

I like it <u>less</u>.

and in expressions: *more or less, less than.*

Activity 3.7

On the following lines decide whether *less* is:

   a. a determiner modifying count nouns. Could *fewer* replace it?
   b. a determiner modifying noncount nouns
   c. an adverb modifying adjectives and adverbs ('negative comparison')
   d. an adverb
   e. a pronoun
   f. an expression.

Hint: decide whether the meaning is 'a smaller amount (of)' or 'to a smaller extent'.

1. Yes, well anyhow, that more or **less** covers the early part of me being on the beat.
2. There will be…**less** distribution issues involved…
3. …neural networks are **less** fashionable than parallel systems at the moment…
4. …no applicant or member of staff will be treated **less** favourably than another…
5. …it's simply a matter of producing a vehicle which uses **less** fuel…
6. Most users believe that the drug is **less** harmful than the tobacco it is rolled with…
7. Rich and famous families usually behave worse than **less** important families…
8. …it sometimes seemed **less** like a current affairs report than an enquiry into a fundamental shift…
9. The policy focuses on using **less** material and energy in the package…
10. …there are now thirty-eight percent **less** people employed than there were a year ago.
11. If recycled materials were used, far **less** energy would be needed, which means **less** pollution.

12. ...there is a tendency to push differences **less** strongly in foreign affairs than in domestic affairs.
13. ...in some cases, costs will be **less** than half that of a leased line.
14. The pair eventually finished in **less** time than many bipeds...
15. It leaves **less** to the discretion of the court...

3.8 *all*

All, referring to the entirety of something, is used in a number of different ways:

- as a determiner with plural count nouns and noncount nouns:

  All roads into the city are closed.
  We've lost all hope.

- as a **predeterminer** preceding definite determiners such as *the*, *his* (**possessive** determiners) or *that* (**demonstrative** determiners):

  All the answers are wrong.

- as a **delayed determiner** to postpone the information given by *all*:

  The ministers have all decided to resign. (cf. *All the ministers...*)

All occupies the **middle** position, as with adverbs. This can happen with objects, especially pronouns, as well as with subjects (as in the above example):

  I'll buy them all a present.

- as a pronoun:

  All I can say is be careful.
  All of the answers are wrong. (= all the answers)

- as an adverb meaning 'completely':

  He lives all alone.

- with singular count nouns *all day/week/year* to refer to entire periods:

  He's been ringing me all day.

- in expressions, for example *at all*:

  I don't understand it at all.

Activity 3.8

Identify whether *all* on these lines is:

  a. a central determiner with a count singular or noncount noun
  b. a predeterminer
  c. a delayed determiner
  d. a pronoun
  e. an adverb modifying an adjective or adverb
  f. part of an expresssion.

Hint: try changing one construction to another, for example *them all* to *all of them*, or vice versa.

1. ...you'll have no problems with them at **all**.
2. Have we got it **all**? Anyone think of anything else?
3. Come on, you're **all** asleep...
4. ...from Saturday my ear was **all** clogged up...
5. You **all** gave us a day to remember...
6. And it goes away and then **all** of a sudden it comes back...
7. This morning I observed **all** of them returning home...
8. I cannot discuss **all** of the essays in the book.
9. **All** prescribed drugs should be in the care of the School Matron.
10. You've been here **all** that time?
11. ...we elect **all** the officers...
12. ...if it had done that to you, it would have been **all** day.
13. But they had **all** their equipment with them...
14. The articles shown in this catalogue are intended for **all** to show their support...
15. Hope you are **all** well.

3.9 *both*

Both has the idea of 'all of the two'. It is used in a number of different ways:

- as a central determiner with plural count nouns:

  Both cases are still under investigation.

- as a predeterminer in front of definite determiners such as *the*, *his* (possessive determiners) or *these* (demonstrative determiners):

  Both these cases are still under investigation.

- as a delayed determiner (cf. *all* in 3.8) to postpone the information given by *both*:

  These cases are both still under investigation.

- as a pronoun:

  As to these cases, both are still under investigation.
  Both of these cases are still under investigation.

- as part of a phrasal **coordinating conjunction** *both...and*, used to emphasise the coordination of two items:

  We're planning to go both today and tomorrow.

Activity 3.9

Decide whether *both* on these lines is a:

a. (central) determiner
b. predeterminer

    c. pronoun
    d. coordinator with *and*
    e. delayed determiner.

Hint: look at the words *both* 'goes with'.

1. However, **both** arguments are spurious…
2. **Both** believe it would be a good idea to slow the momentum…
3. **Both** could be kept within bounds by a severe pruning in early spring.
4. Huge amounts of information can now be…sent in **both** directions along television cables.
5. …it will become the common database for **both** environments.
6. I was privy to all their discussions on Hardy, as **both** had known him…
7. Ordinary wild plants…are weedier than crops, but **both** have a long way to go to catch up with the real pests.
8. In **both** June and November, about two-thirds of the absentee pupils were absent…
9. …**both** of these organisms have prominent adhesion mechanisms.
10. I think it applies to **both** sexes.
11. …so I think it's got to be looked at from **both** sides.
12. …they are **both** the same age, aren't they?
13. It would seem that at the police station Mr. Bell denied **both** those matters.
14. Another example is the use of **both** urban and agricultural wastes…
15. Those proceedings were concluded on 19 January 1988 when **both** were acquitted.

3.10 every

Compared to other determiners, *every* is a straightforward word grammatically since it is never used as a pronoun or adverb. However, although it is usually used with singular count nouns, its meaning is plural; for example:

> You should seize *every* opportunity.

If it is important not to mention the noun, *every one* can be used:

> We gave him several choices but he refused *every one*.

This is not to be confused with the compound pronoun *everyone*, which only refers to people:

> *Everyone* is welcome to join the party.

The main difference in meaning between *every* and *all* is that *every* allows members of a group to be considered separately, while *all* refers to the whole group. For instance, in the following example it would be difficult to use *all*:

> For *every* person who leaves Paris, two move to the suburbs.

It is commonly used with time expressions to indicate regular intervals of time:

> *Every week* they got a rest day.

Sometimes the following noun phrase appears to be plural:

An earthquake might occur <u>every</u> <u>100 years</u>.

But this is referring to a 100-year period.

Every is also used:

- with **abstract** nouns, to express a positive attitude to an idea:

She had <u>every reason</u> to expect help.

- in expressions such as *every so often*, *every now and then*, indicating regularly occurring events;
- as a part of the conjunction *every time* (*that*), meaning the same as 'whenever':

<u>Every time</u> you go away…

Activity 3.10

On the following lines decide whether *every* is:

a. followed by an abstract noun
b. followed by a noun referring to a time period
c. part of a conjunction
d. not followed by a noun

Hint: try replacing *every* with *all* and make other necessary changes.

1. Intensive courses start **every** 4 weeks.
2. He…insists that **every** child ought to be a wanted child.
3. **Every** clinic conducts regular surveys to monitor the effects of the programme.
4. …but I hope all members living locally will make **every** effort to come…
5. …on your behalf I want to wish her **every** happiness in her new life…
6. The experiment gave **every** indication that this would be possible…
7. We hold special events **every** month…
8. …it's not something you can just apply **every** now and again.
9. …it is for **every** one of us!
10. …**every** patient expects that the doctor knows all about them…
11. [They] are more likely to wear watches so that they can make **every** second count.
12. And I'm falling asleep **every** time I sit down.

3.11 *few*

Few can be compared and contrasted with *little*. Their relationship is the same as that between *many* and *much*. As a determiner *few* is used with plural count nouns, with the idea of 'not many'; for example:

<u>Few experiences</u> can beat watching the sun rise from the top of a mountain.

In another respect, *few* and *little* are similar: both can be preceded by *a* to give a more positive impression:

<u>A few</u> questions won't do any harm.

It is also used as a pronoun:

Few would disagree with you.

In this context it sounds formal (as it does in the example above as a determiner); *not many* would be more normal. Like *many* it is not used as an adverb.

Few is often preceded by intensifiers:

There are <u>very</u> few opportunities nowadays for graduates.

Activity 3.11

a. First, identify whether *few* is being used as a determiner or a pronoun.

b. Second, decide where *a* could be added to change the impression from negative to positive.

Hint: work out where *not many* could replace *few*.

1. Second, while two thirds of respondents espoused an open systems policy, in reality **few** are adopting it…
2. And it wasn't a case of just a **few** beatings…
3. [He] was wondering whether we might want to go out for a **few** beers…
4. …for the next **few** days Anne planned what she would put in her cake.
5. Here are a **few** of his original concepts and time-saving techniques…
6. There are **few** people who have had a more unique opportunity…
7. Very **few** people at all would ever…say that…
8. …a **few** pubs, often in rural areas, keep their casks on or behind the bar…
9. A **few** receive the justice that has been denied to them for five centuries…
10. An estimate of numbers was impossible in the **few** seconds available at the pause…
11. …an update to overcome the problem should be in place in a **few** weeks' time.
12. I'd like, if I may, to say a **few** words on behalf of the…Foundation.

Chapter 4

Adjectives

4.0 Introduction

Adjectives are a significant word class but individually they are not as frequent as function words. The words presented below have been chosen to be representative of the most important factors affecting adjectives. These include their position in structure and the words they frequently co-occur with.

The first distinction to be made is between the attributive and predicative use of adjectives. An attributive adjective is one that precedes the **head noun** in a noun phrase as its **premodification**: *a red dress*. There may be more than one adjective: *a beautiful red dress*.

A predicative adjective is one that is used on its own, separate from a noun, typically after the verb *be*: *her dress is red*, but also after other so-called **link verbs**: *I feel great*. Here, it functions as the **predicative** element in a clause.

Some adjectives occur only as attributive adjectives: *the main argument* (not **the argument is main*) and some only as predicative adjectives: *the people are afraid* (not **the afraid people*). The reason underlying this is that in the attributive position the adjective refers to some lasting characteristic, whereas in the predicative position the adjective refers to a temporary state. That is why *happy*, as well as predicatively, can be used attributively (*happy people*) – while *glad* cannot (**glad people*).

Sometimes there is a difference in meaning between the attributive and predicative use of one adjective. Compare *my mother is late* with *my late* (= 'dead') *mother*.

A third way in which the position of adjectives in structure is important is when they occur as the head of a noun phrase preceded by *the*, referring in general to all people with that characteristic:

> *The rich have had it too easy up to now.*

This 'generic' use applies to a fairly limited number of adjectives such as *the handicapped, the sick, the young*.

Another important factor is the words that adjectives tend to occur with. Thus, a lot of adjectives are said to be 'gradable' in that various levels of its characteristic are possible. This is shown when **degree adverbs** are placed in front: *very good, quite good, how good*, etc. Some adjectives are not gradable because their quality is a matter of yes or no. For example, *main* or *national*; you cannot say **very main* or **so national*.

Also important with adjectives is what comes after them. Some are closely attached to a following preposition when they are used predicatively:

He's afraid of snakes.
They're dependent on handouts.

These prepositional phrases are sometimes called 'adjective complements'. Some predicative adjectives have to be followed by one in order to make the meaning complete:

I'm particularly fond of sheep cheese. (you cannot say *I'm particularly fond. What of?)

Adjective complements involving other constructions (i.e. not just prepositional phrases) are possible; for example, **to infinitives**:

I'm pleased to meet you.

There are some adjectives which have an obligatory complement with a *to* infinitive:

We have classes for people who are unable to join our ordinary groups.

Another common adjective complement is a subordinate clause starting with *that*:

I'm glad that you two are back together.

A final factor to consider is adjectives which end in *-ed* and *-ing*; for example, *satisfying* and *satisfied*. These are historically derived from the formally identical **-ed** and **-ing participles** but are used differently, so it is necessary to distinguish their adjectival and verbal uses:

That meal was very satisfying. (adjective)
I've been satisfying their demands all day. (verb)
I am satisfied with her answers. (adjective)
Our curiosity has been satisfied. (verb)

One factor that is not dealt with here is the issue of how these adjectives form their **comparatives** and **superlatives** (e.g. *big, bigger, biggest*) since this involves a change of form, and, as with other inflections, this is beyond the scope of this book.

Adjectives are quite straightforward in their uses. Normally they are only adjectives (though there are some exceptions below), and what is of interest is the different category of adjective they belong to and their structural behaviour with other words.

Most of the following sections do not outline their different uses; these are already described above. The activities simply invite the reader to evaluate the words according to those factors. Except in the last two sections, instead of an 'answer', there is a comment by way of conclusion.

4.1 brave

Activity 4.1

Evaluate these lines for *brave* according to the factors in 4.0.

1. It is an activity of the **brave** and strong and not of the cowardly...
2. ...it's a very **brave** doctor who will then say absolutely no!
3. When friends came to stay we put on a **brave** face...
4. He stirs a band of **brave** knights to tackle the rising army of the dead...
5. His story tells of the **brave** men of the New Zealand Shipping Co Tekoa.
6. It was a dangerous and extremely **brave** thing to do.

7. …who's feeling very **brave** this morning?
8. **Brave** though he is in facing adult audiences, the result is a bit of a cringe…
9. Ha, she said, and laughed back as though trying to be **brave**, trying to be strong.
10. He was **brave** until the very last moment.
11. And the winner of a mass sprint is a **brave** winner indeed.
12. …this means suppressing a growing number of **brave** young people whose only crime is to write a leaflet…

4.2 *homeless*

Activity 4.2

Analyse the following lines for *homeless* according to the factors in 4.0.

1. The plaintiff and his family were **homeless** and in priority need of accommodation.
2. …the local authority had wrongly decided that he was intentionally **homeless**.
3. It also showed the typical daily diets…of the **homeless** in Britain.
4. …these are the most important things we can offer to those who are **homeless**…
5. Approaching 1,000 **homeless** men have been temporarily housed there…
6. …over 1,000 students are involved in areas of work with the local community such as running a shelter for the **homeless** or teaching an adult to read.
7. …we also give advice and support to **homeless** people…
8. As you have been informed, my council makes one offer only to **homeless** persons.
9. [They run] a soup kitchen for London's **homeless**…
10. Long-term projects include support to the Aberdeen Cyrenians who help **homeless** young people…

4.3 *poor*

Activity 4.3

Analyse the following lines for *poor* according to the factors in 4.0. Also check the meanings according to the different uses.

1. …people living in **poor** locations could no longer feed themselves…
2. However, mothers…attribute a bewildering variety of symptoms to teething, including **poor** sleeping…
3. All of that gives it a very encouraging sure-footedness once you…test it on **poor** road conditions.
4. Lunchtime drinking that leads to reduced or **poor** quality work in the afternoons is one example.
5. Paul Cook's **poor** pass let in Martin Carruthers.
6. …we haven't got a clue what the **poor** girl's doing at the moment.
7. …I think we are economically and industrially the **poor** men of Europe…
8. Let's have a look in and see what you've done to the **poor** old thing.
9. Hence, the priesthood…must exhibit a preferential love for the **poor**…
10. What have you done to this **poor** wee man?
11. …this was probably due to **poor** note-keeping rather than a percentage.

12. The survey also showed that many people are eating a very **poor** diet.
13. ...when there is a very **poor** harvest prices rocket through the roof...
14. ...peasants were being heavily taxed and harvests were **poor**...
15. ...all his friends were **poor** too.

4.4 *mere*

Mere has the idea of 'only', except that it is an adjective while *only* is an adverb.

Activity 4.4

Analyse the following lines for *mere* according to the factors in 4.0. Also check the meanings according to the different uses.

1. The flower...lasted a **mere** 18 hours before it wilted.
2. One indicator is the fact that a **mere** 3,660 votes were cast for the candidate...
3. A **mere** 8 percent think British schools are superior.
4. We won't ever be wealthy, but the **mere** fact that we ARE working means that we must be healthy...
5. A **mere** handful set up their own business.
6. ...journalists strive earnestly to shed their previous role as **mere** mouthpieces of dictatorial regimes...
7. His deep sense of his own sinful heart was no **mere** passing emotion...
8. ...**mere** seconds might mean the difference between life and death...
9. [They] said connections with other incidents was **mere** speculation.
10. ...the head would hang on quite a while by a **mere** thread.

4.5 *former*

Former has two meanings. In one it is opposed to *latter* in picking out the first of two things already mentioned in a text. In the other more common meaning it refers to something that used to be: *a former boyfriend*.

Activity 4.5

Analyse the following lines for *former* according to the factors in 4.0. Also check the meanings according to the different uses.

1. The first of these columns is very much in the **former** category and will appear in the next issue.
2. His second reaction was gut terror that his **former** comrades would come looking for him.
3. Stephen Bayley, **former** director of the Design Museum, will chair a debate...
4. The clinic is situated...at a **former** farmhouse on the Closkelt Road...
5. The **former** has the difficulty of selection of what is relevant...
6. When their secondment did come to an end, 22 returned to their **former** jobs...
7. For them it was a case of re-attachment to the **former** post and detachment from the secondment.

8. ...he is a **former** president of the RSS...
9. Ms Rainford is a **former** pupil of Marymount and Upton Hall convent schools.
10. My colleagues are willing to join me in concerts in several cities in the **former** Yugoslavia.

4.6 *ill*

Ill is often cited as an example of a predicative-only adjective; for instance, you talk about *a sick person* rather than *an ill person*.

Activity 4.6

Look at the lines below to see how far this is true.

1. Paul will want to remember their Mummy as she was before she got **ill**...
2. [She] is determined to improve standards of care for mentally **ill** and handicapped people.
3. ...it made an exception of the mentally **ill** because of the pressing need to act swiftly.
4. On this and the previous day I was **ill**, but was able to attend the closing meeting...
5. But you don't have to swallow the water to become **ill**.
6. The guests...were lectured on his concern for the **ill** effects of Western food on the health of Europeans...
7. Father was very **ill**, he had TB, and during the war he became worse...
8. Though dogged by **ill** health in later years he was still able to work...
9. Nearly all interviewees claimed they had been forced to cut down on food and fuel and many reported **ill** health.
10. Last week I was quite **ill**...
11. District nurses have always had the skills to treat acutely **ill** patients...
12. Sometimes, when you are **ill**, the doctor comes to your home.
13. ...just because she is disabled, it does not mean she is medically **ill**.
14. If people got seriously **ill**, we had to carry them back...
15. I was awfully **ill** with it last night.

4.7 *ready*

Ready is normally only used predicatively.

Activity 4.7

Analyse the following lines for *ready* according to the factors in 4.0. In particular check what kind of adjective complements are used when *ready* is predicative.

1. See if we can get her **ready** for the dancing.
2. The vast bulk of enterprises are not **ready** for change.
3. Ah, that's not **ready** for opening yet...
4. Many apples and pears are now **ready** for picking...
5. If the people were **ready** for negotiations, he wouldn't be against it.

6. ...you won't be **ready** from the latest report.
7. The priest...must be genuine and brotherly, and always **ready** to understand...
8. [It] is now independent and is **ready** to break away from its tobacco brand association...
9. After five years, Josiah was **ready** to set up in business on his own account...
10. I developed a very bad throat and could not fly, just before we were **ready** to leave for overseas...
11. Come on, be **ready**.
12. After that, it was a mad dash to get **ready**.

4.8 *happy*

Activity 4.8

Evaluate the following lines for *happy* according to the factors in 4.0. In particular, note the complements when it is used predicatively.

1. I'm not **happy** about the way they've drawn up the writ...
2. It was a **happy**, friendly and very satisfying day...
3. If he is not **happy**, the patient should contact the manufacturer.
4. ...we are **happy** to answer any queries about our own products...
5. ...we will be **happy** to make arrangements in advance for anyone unable to go upstairs.
6. I'd be **happy** to keep you going for a bit longer.
7. ...we were only too **happy** to oblige.
8. ...if you could maybe refer me I would be **happy** with that.
9. ...the client is more than **happy** with his choice of lawyer.
10. She is surprised, but **very** happy.

4.9 *fond*

Fond, like *ill*, is sometimes said to be an example of an adjective that must be used predicatively, and therefore must always be followed by a prepositional complement beginning with *of* (see 5.0).

Activity 4.9

Look at the lines below and examine these two claims.

1. ...the 34-year-old American waved a **fond** farewell to the big-time...
2. ...they did it out of their **fond** love for her...
3. There will be many **fond** memories taken away from the city...
4. ...police are **fond** of saying publicly that they want to build bridges with the community here.
5. He said he felt no pain, apart from injections which he has never been **fond** of...
6. He's obviously **fond** of women.
7. I'm not too **fond** of taking tablets...
8. I am very **fond** of poetry by John Donne.
9. He was very **fond** of ancient histories, stories and epics of earlier times and heroes.

10. He was **fond** of saying that he could not have done any of it without June…
11. He asked them to make drawings, and compared these with the artwork kept by **fond** parents…
12. Many…celebrities added anecdotes to the **fond** reminiscences of family and friends…

4.10 *aware*

Aware is sometimes said to be always used predicatively and with complements (typically beginning with *of* or *that*).

Activity 4.10

On the lines below check a) the different complements *aware* is used with and whether it always has one, and b) whether it can be used attributively:

1. [The] scheme would enable staff to become **aware** and provide assistance to users.
2. I am **aware** of the difficult times that other theatre companies actually face…
3. Just…be **aware** of what sugary foods and drinks can do to your teeth.
4. I became **aware** of an angry bee searching frantically for the entrance to its hive.
5. In recent years people have become increasingly **aware** of the foods they consume…
6. Nowadays everybody is **aware** of how important it is to be fit.
7. Teachers are often not **aware** of the possibilities…
8. …it's something to be slightly **aware** of…
9. Vulnerable people should be **aware** that there are some laboratories and practitioners who rely on controversial and unproven procedures…
10. I wasn't **aware** that it was actually used [in such a way].
11. …they are only **aware** that the blanket of fear is suddenly not so suffocating any more.
12. [It] campaigns relentlessly for a…politically more **aware** world.

4.11 *late*

Late generally means 'behind in time', and it can be used both attributively and predicatively:

> *Late arrivals will not be admitted.*
> *You're late again.*

However, there are other meanings which can only apply attributively, for example; when it is used as a euphemism for 'dead':

> *I miss the late King very much.* (Not *the King is late.*)

or when it refers to the latter part of a period:

> *My favourite time is the late afternoon.* (Not *the afternoon is late.*)

Another point to consider is that *late* can also be an adverb: *they arrived late*. It is not related to the adverb *lately* which means 'recently'.

Activity 4.11

Identify on these lines where:

   a. *late* is used attributively;
   b. its meaning is restricted to attributive use;
   c. it is an adverb.

  1. The system was developed by a Japanese academic in the **late** 1800s...
  2. **Late** applicants are also invited to participate in this selection seminar...
  3. Unfortunately the service may come too **late** for a childless woman...
  4. I had occasion in **late** October to present a brief profile of Havel...
  5. They all just came back for a regular routine follow up, just a little bit **late**.
  6. ...every effort is made to offer those who book **late** the course they have requested...
  7. ...inflation is expected to accelerate towards 7.5 per cent **late** this year...
  8. Deliveries, they warn, are likely to be a little **late** this year...
  9. ...it's a bit **late** to do those today I'm afraid.
 10. He and his **late** wife...owned two properties as beneficial joint tenants...

4.12 old

Old, like *late*, is an adjective with several meanings, one of which can only occur attributively, namely when it is used as a term of affection:

> *Have you seen <u>old</u> John lately?*

It does not always mean 'advanced in years'.

Activity 4.12

On the lines below identify:

   a. where *old* is used attributively;
   b. where its meaning is restricted to attributive use as a term of affection;
   c. one line (described in 4.0) where it is neither attributive nor predicative.

  1. This luxury six-court development provides for every player's needs, whether beginner, advanced, young or **old**.
  2. You must be getting **old**.
  3. The **old** battleship Rodney was rolling along nicely.
  4. Make sure that you...dispose of **old** fridges carefully.
  5. The **old** homestead has been gutted.
  6. ...she reiterated her **old** misgivings about the monetary system...
  7. Let's have a listen to you and see what you're doing to your poor **old** self...
  8. [She] can make the **old** weep when she sings Roses of Picardy...

4.13 *satisfied*

The last two adjectives in this chapter are different from the previous ones, in that they are related to verbs (although most of the same features still apply). *Satisfied* is related to the verb, *satisfy*, from whose **-ed participle** it is derived and with which it shares the same form. It can be very difficult to distinguish the two, particularly when the adjective is used predicatively after a form of the verb *be*, since this looks the same as a passive form of the verb:

> We <u>were</u> <u>satisfied</u> with her work. (adjective)
> We <u>were</u> <u>satisfied</u> by her answer. (*-ed* participle, part of a passive)

There is a small but important difference in meaning: the adjective refers to a state, whereas the verb refers to an action.

Activity 4.13

On the lines below work out whether *satisified* is:

a. a predicative adjective
b. an *-ed* participle.

Also identify the different complements that follow the adjective.

Hint: try replacing *satisfied* with a similar-meaning adjective such as *happy*, or try placing *very* in front of it to see if it a gradable adjective.

1. In France, honour is **satisfied** by a low-level court case taking half an hour.
2. Most schools seemed to be **satisfied** that they were meeting the needs of pupils…
3. We are **satisfied** the agreement is enforceable.
4. …it seems that he was **satisfied** with my performance in the interview…
5. I was very **satisfied** with the arrangements for accommodation.
6. …do you think the women are **satisfied** with the kind of provisions that there are made for them…?
7. The Government Railway Inspector was generally **satisfied** with the trials…
8. Requests…should normally be **satisfied** within thirty minutes.

4.14 *amusing*

Like *satisfied*, *amusing* is an adjective related to a verb, *amuse*, from whose **-ing participle** it is derived and with which it shares the same form. It can be difficult to distinguish the two, particularly when the adjective is used predicatively after a form of the verb *be*, since this looks the same as the **progressive** forms of the verb:

> Their jokes are frustrating but <u>amusing</u>. (adjective)
> They are <u>amusing</u> us with their jokes. (*-ing* participle, part of a progressive)

There is also a small but important difference in meaning: the adjective refers to a state, the verb to an action. As a verb, *amuse* is monotransitive (see Chapter 7), so there is an object (*us*) in the second example. As an adjective, *amusing* is gradable, so degree adverbs may be used with it: …*frustrating but very amusing.*

Activity 4.14

Identify on the following lines whether *amusing* is:

  a.   an attributive adjective
  b.   a predicative adjective
  c.   an *-ing* participle.

Hint: look for a degree adverb or try to insert one, or look for an object.

  1.   ...perhaps it wasn't so **amusing** after all.
  2.   PS. I did find the article **amusing**...
  3.   They are very colourful and **amusing** characters.
  4.   I have probably seen less **amusing** comedies than this...
  5.   I thought it was all very **amusing**.
  6.   Jokes can become more **amusing** if you can perfect the appropriate accent...
  7.   ...in fact, it's quite **amusing** in some ways...
  8.   How **amusing** it was to watch this young man, he thought.
  9.   Staff in the department all find it highly **amusing**...
  10. I know you've got some other **amusing** stories...
  11. ...they looked like they were **amusing** themselves at a family party...
  12. ...it is portrayed in a very **amusing** way in this film by Woody Allen...

Chapter 5

Prepositions

5.0 Introduction

Prepositions are some of the most frequent words in English; all those included here are in the top 100, and *of*, *to* and *in* are in the top 10. They are a **closed** word class, in that their number is limited, and it is not easy to make new members. As such, they are counted among the **function** words of English, having a grammatical role and sometimes containing little or no meaning.

They have two main functions in grammar:

1. to introduce **prepositional phrases** which operate independently as **adverbials** in clauses:

> *She was standing <u>on the corner</u>.*
> *We'll meet up <u>at 9</u>.*
> *I opened it <u>with my pen</u>.*
> *I did it <u>for no reason</u>.*

Here, they answer questions such as *Where* (*was she standing?*), *When* (*will we meet up?*) and *How* (*did you open it?*), as well as *Why* (*did you do it?*). As such, they refer to basic meanings of place, time, manner, cause and reason, and a whole range of other meanings (indicated below in the sections). To take prepositions of place as an example, we can identify a basic triad of *in* (whose noun phrase has the idea of a container), *on* (surface) and *at* (point). It is sometimes assumed that specific nouns always take the same preposition (e.g. *on the floor* = surface), and this can be reinforced by gap-filling exercises, but a certain amount of speaker choice is possible. That is why you can be both *on a bus* (a surface) and *in a bus* (a container), or *at a place* as well as *in a place*.

2. to relate **noun phrases** to preceding **nouns**, **adjectives** and **verbs**: *the daughter of the king.*

Here, their meaning is less obvious. For example, *of* is often said to refer to possession, but in fact it covers a wide range of relationships (as with the above example; the king does not 'own' the daughter), and in some cases it serves a grammatical function (see 5.1 below). Sometimes prepositions are very closely related to the preceding words (and may be determined by it); for example:

- with nouns:

It had a great effect on me.
A belief in humanity can often be harmful.

- with adjectives:

I'm proud of you.

The prepositional phrases following nouns and adjectives in such cases are sometimes called noun/adjective **complements**, and they form part of the **postmodification** of the noun or adjective.

- with verbs, in what are called 'prepositional verbs' (see Chapter 9 on Multi-word verbs), e.g. *look after, rely on*:

They'll look after the cats while we're away.

It is hard to say that these prepositions have any particular meaning. With noun and adjective complements, comparable verb forms often have no preposition (e.g. *It affected me greatly*). With prepositional verbs the meaning is idiomatic; in other words, it cannot be guessed from the two parts.

Prepositions are always part of prepositional phrases (except *to* in one situation; see 5.2 below). However, in certain circumstances they can be 'stranded', that is, separated from their noun phrase; for example:

- in some relative clauses:

It's not the pain that I'm afraid of. (…afraid of the pain)

- in passives with prepositional verbs:

The case is being looked into. (Someone is looking into the case)

Prepositions may also occur as part of longer **multi-word prepositions**; for example, *of* in *in front of, in spite of*.

5.1 *of*

Of is the most frequent preposition; it is rare to find a sentence that does not include it. It indicates a wide range of relationships between noun phrases, not just possession or ownership as is commonly maintained.

It commonly introduces prepositional phrases which function as a **postmodifer** in **noun phrases**:

the Chairman of the Board
the corner of the room
the aim of the game

Note that none of these indicate possession.

Of can also have a grammatical function to indicate underlying subject/verb or verb/object relationships:

> The release *of* the prisoner... (verb/object; they released the prisoner)
> The decision *of* the court... (subject/verb; the court decided...)

This process of making noun phrases out of underlying verb relationships is sometimes called 'nominalisation'.

In the cases above, the use of *of* is similar to the use of the **genitive**, and often both are possible:

> the Board's Chairman
> the game's aim
> the prisoner's release
> the court's decision

But, sometimes the alternative sounds strange: ?*the room's corner*. There are many factors which determine the choice between *of* and the genitive; one is the length of the postmodifying noun phrase. For example:

> The end of this long-running serial...

would sound strange as:

> ?This long-running serial's end...

One common relationship between noun phrases indicated by *of* is 'consisting of':

> I've had years *of* practice.

Here, *of* could also be paraphrased loosely by 'amounting to' or 'involving'. An alternative with a genitive is not possible here.

Another common use of *of* is in 'quantifying expressions', following **quantifiers** such as *most/many/much/a lot/few/little/some/all* (these were considered to be pronouns grammatically in Chapter 3):

> Much of what he said made no sense. (Or A lot of...)

These constructions are sometimes called 'partitives'.

There are situations where *of* does not relate two noun phrases:

- following adjectives, where it forms an adjective complement with the noun phrase:

> They are very fond of their grandchildren.

- in prepositional verbs (see section 5.0 and Chapter 9 for more on this):

> This book consists of 12 chapters.

Of also occurs in multi-word prepositions: *out of, because of, on top of, in front of, in spite of,* and in expressions: *of course*.

Activity 5.1a

On the lines below turn the *of* phrase into a genitive and decide whether:

a. it is possible
b. it sounds strange
c. it makes no sense.

Hint: use your intuitions.

1. In the course **of** the book Nash seems to adopt a rather detached stance…
2. …since the War London has been the centre **of** the recording industry…
3. So, to meet the demands **of** the diesel boom, oil companies have installed diesel pumps…
4. A friend **of** the band weaved in and out of the crowd…
5. Green…repeatedly wonders about the identity **of** the first-person speaker…
6. The level **of** tuition fees charged to students gives them the right…
7. The primary function **of** the teacher is…to help the student to assimilate the course…
8. …usually the more dominant member **of** the clan is the oldest.
9. This table is only a very general point **of** reference.
10. Next Tuesday it's the turn **of** drama and literature…
11. The growth **of** a tumour is regulated both by the rate at which its cells divide…
12. Well it's a nice part **of** the world.

Activity 5.1b

Decide whether *of* on these lines:

Hint: look at the words preceding *of*.

a. is part of a quantifying expression;
b. means 'consist of';
c. is part of a prepositional verb;
d. is part of an expression or multi-word preposition;
e. indicates an underlying verbal relationship (verb + object);
f. is part of an adjective complement.

1. The European region consists **of** three main groups…
2. …it never does to show these people how frightened you are **of** them…
3. His book starts, for instance, by making…sense out **of** a nonsense letter of Lear's…
4. Vauxhall announced on May 28 that all 5,128 **of** its UK Corsas were being recalled because **of** an electrical fault.
5. …we lapse into a silent vocabulary **of** eye and hand, a collusion **of** smiles…
6. …so she gave me a couple **of** tablets.
7. …there is no discussion **of** the many features…in the text.
8. The initial appointment is for one year but may be cancelled in the event **of** a serious breach of the guidelines…
9. His customers were not buying fuel but the…memories **of** childhood story books.

10. I marked the entrance to the hive with three blobs **of** paint of a different colour...
11. ...the disposal and site maintenance is also costing us a lot **of** money...
12. A small theatre group takes on the task **of** mounting a Passion Play...
13. Have we got it all? Anyone think **of** anything else?
14. Alternative medicine practitioners were accused...**of** making false and misleading claims...
15. It is a beautiful piece **of** technology and science...
16. ...important progress was made in the use **of** new machinery, the introduction **of** the first coloured earthenware bodies and the manufacture **of** bone china...
17. They warn that a fourth year **of** drought will further hit farmers...
18. ...there seems to be little evidence yet **of** any change in common practice...

5.2 to

While all the other words in this chapter are used solely as prepositions, as part of prepositional phrases, *to* is also used in a very different role: as a marker of **infinitives**.

Infinitives preceded by *to* can be contrasted with bare infinitives. The latter are generally restricted to modal auxiliaries (see Chapter 8):

Can you wait for a while?

and to a few main verbs such as *make* and verbs of perception:

They made us do it.
Have you ever heard her laugh?

To infinitives are generally used with main verbs:

I want to go.
We've decided to stay.

and with semi-modals such as *have to, have got to, be able to, used to, ought to*:

You have to leave now.
We used to go there every weekend.

(See Chapter 8 for more on modals and semi-modals.) There may be an object intervening between the verb and the infinitive:

I want you to leave immediately.

but the infinitive is still determined by the verb.

To infinitives may also be triggered by a noun or adjective, as part of their complement:

They made a decision to continue with the renovation.
The students are afraid to go out.

There is also the so-called **infinitive of purpose** where the infinitive phrase can be questioned with *why...?*:

It should be applied daily to be effective.

Here, the text could be made more explicit with the addition of 'in order':...*in order to be effective.*

As a preposition, *to* has the basic meaning of direction or destination:

> *I cycle <u>to work</u> every day.*

Here, the prepositional phrase functions as an adverbial and answers the question *Where… (to)?*

The other main use of *to* as a preposition is to indicate the person or persons who are recipients of some action:

> *I wrote a letter <u>to all the parents of the children involved</u>.*

The prepositional phrase beginning with *to* is sometimes called a 'prepositional object'; it answers the question *Who…to?* or *To whom…?* Such prepositional objects can be related to indirect objects without *to*:

> *I wrote <u>the parents</u> a letter.*

Prepositional *to* also occurs:

- in noun and adjective complements:

> *This has no <u>relevance</u> <u>to our discussion</u>.*
> *My sister isn't at all <u>similar</u> <u>to me</u>.*

- in prepositional verbs (see Chapter 9):

> *This doesn't <u>apply to</u> us.*

This needs to be distinguished from the adverbial and prepositional object uses described above. It does not relate to a question with *where* and, although it may be considered a prepositional object (*Who does it apply to?*), it is not related to an indirect object.

- in phrasal verbs (see Chapter 9):

> *When she <u>came to</u>, there was no one in the room.*

- in multi-word prepositions, such as *according to* and *due to*.

Activity 5.2a

First of all, identify all the infinitives on the lines below. Then distinguish these uses according to whether they are:

a. necessitated by a preceding semi-modal
b. necessitated by a preceding adjective or noun to introduce a complement
c. necessitated by a preceding main verb.

Hint: look at the words preceding *to*.

1. …they are confident they will be able **to** match up the bulb for you.
2. The tax take varies according **to** the retail price.

3. The burning of waste is another thing which adds **to** the Greenhouse effect…
4. I'm in the right place **to** twist an arm.
5. This encompasses all ranges of ability from the beginner **to** the very experienced.
6. Now the university has decided **to** spend one hundred and fifty thousand pounds…
7. These complex substances are then very difficult **to** remove in the drinking water production process.
8. …where glazing or a doorway extends **to** ceiling height, it may be necessary **to** terminate the cove…
9. Okay, sit, sit still, be quiet and listen **to** this…
10. Your supporter's reference number will appear on the address label of our next mailing **to** you.
11. The current system of taxation of alcoholic drinks is unnecessarily complicated **to** administer…
12. And I think that's what we ought **to** use.
13. …three Beluga whales, which are closely related **to** dolphins, had made their own bid for freedom.
14. You've got **to** keep checking the level.
15. I think it's really relevant **to** the pictures…
16. It brought tears **to** my eyes when I heard that the house would be closed…
17. …some people are trying **to** press ahead with their moves before Christmas…
18. The news…brought a new sense of unease **to** the inhabitants…
19. I mean we've got a friend and she used **to** smoke sixty a day…
20. I still want **to** have the downward trend…

Activity 5.2b

Using the same lines, but excluding all the lines where it marks an infinitive identified in Activity 5.2.a, decide whether *to*:

a. introduces a prepositional complement after a noun or adjective;
b. is part of a prepositional verb;
c. introduces an adverbial;
d. introduces a prepositional object;
e. is part of a multi-word preposition.

Hint: look at the words before and after *to*.

5.3 *in*

In introduces prepositional phrase which either function as adverbials:

> Costs are much lower <u>in the north</u>.

or as the postmodification of a noun:

> Costs <u>in the north</u> are much lower.
> I noticed a <u>man</u> <u>in a leather jacket</u>.

In terms of meaning, the prepositional phrase indicates location or place, with the idea of the preceding noun phrase being contained. This idea of 'containment' can apply physically to places and locations:

She is now in the building.
They live in London.

It can also apply metaphorically to periods of time:

We met in 2009.

and the manner of actions:

They performed the song in great style.

Referring to time, *in* can also mean a point in the future at the end of a period:

Term starts in three weeks.

When used as an adverbial, the prepositional phrase can be questioned using *where* and *when* and *how*:

Where is she now?
Where do they live?
When did we meet?
When does term start?
How did they perform the song?

In can also be used:

- in prepositional verbs (see Chapter 9):

  I don't believe in ghosts.

- in phrasal verbs (see Chapter 9):

  If it's too big we can take it in.

- in noun complements:

  I have no confidence in their ability.

- as an adverb meaning 'at home':

  I wasn't in when they called.

- in a number of expressions: *in fact, in order to*, etc.

Activity 5.3

On the lines below decide whether *in*:

a. introduces an adverbial referring to place;
b. introduces an adverbial referring to time;

   c. introduces an adverbial referring to manner;
   d. is part of an expression;
   e. is part of a phrasal verb.

Hint: ask questions with *where*, *when* and *how* replacing the prepositional phrase.

1. The other area that we explored **in** some depth was…
2. The future is **in** your hands…
3. …we'll have more sessions booked **in** tomorrow…
4. We wanted people to enjoy an afternoon **in** the pub without alcohol…
5. **In** another incident, patients had been given fake steroid creams, he added.
6. This, **in** turn, is part of an issue which will be devoted entirely to papers on typography.
7. …I suspect that Blake is influenced **in** his choice by his misleading view…
8. [She] said the building should be open **in** July…
9. Champagne is a designation used only for sparkling wine produced **in** the limited area of Northern France around the towns of Reims…
10. This material is protected…and may not be copied or redistributed **in** any way.
11. …you keep hearing reports **in** the medical journals about doctors being sued…
12. …various approaches may be as valid as that **in** the solutions. You should, **in** general, use the printed solution…

5.4 *on*

On is typically used to introduce prepositional phrases which function as adverbials. In terms of meaning, it can refer to locations, with the idea of a surface:

   We found it <u>on the beach</u>.

or dates:

   They arrived <u>on New Year's Eve</u>.

It can also be used:

- in phrasal verbs (see Chapter 9):

   Could you <u>turn</u> the light <u>on</u>?

- in prepositional verbs (see Chapter 9):

   You can <u>rely on</u> me.

- in noun and adjective complements:

   We'll release a <u>statement on</u> this tomorrow.
   The babies are <u>dependent on</u> their mothers for everything.

Activity 5.4

On the following lines decide whether *on*:

    a. introduces an adverbial indicating location;
    b. introduces an adverbial indicating a date;
    c. is part of a noun complement;
    d. is part of a prepositional verb.

Hint: try replacing the prepositional phrase beginning *in…* with *here*, *there* or *then*.

1. Exhibitions, educational films, period plays, even music, are all **on** the agenda…
2. Webster died **on** 21 April 1988.
3. Nearly all interviewees claimed they had been forced to cut down **on** food and fuel…
4. He will advise management **on** such issues…
5. Nescafé was off the menu **on** Wednesday…
6. The play takes place **on** two sides of the Atlantic…
7. But after the publicity **on** unleaded fuel there has been increased interest…
8. A recent BBC documentary **on** the subject showed the dramatic results achieved…
9. This means that there will be no restriction **on** the number of places available…
10. Mr. Gilbert, the complainant, gave evidence that **on** the evening of 22 April 1990 he was in a public house.
11. Speaking French can be useful **on** holiday…
12. …he had written a document setting out his views **on** negotiations…

5.5 *for*

For is often said to refer to a person who benefits from something. However, when used to introduce prepositional phrases functioning as adverbials, it has a wide range of possible meanings, answering various questions:

- duration/time periods, answering the questions 'for how long?':

  He's been a senator for thirty years.

- reasons, answering the question 'why?':

  She was arrested for assault.

- purpose, answering the question 'what…for?':

  Water is for drinking.

- representation, answering the question 'what/who…for?':

  She's the admissions officer for the English Department.

- benefit, answering the question 'who…for?':

  They did it for me.

In some cases the prepositional phrase is equivalent in meaning to an **indirect object**:

What can I get you/get for you?
Can I get something for you? Can I get you something?

For is also used in the following circumstances:

- in prepositional verbs:

What are you looking for in life?

- to introduce the complement of a noun:

Some people have a need for success. (= 'they need success')

- as a rather formal conjunction similar to *since* to express a reason:

The journey troubled him for he had never set foot outside his country.

- in expressions such as *for example, for instance*.

Activity 5.5

On the following lines decide whether *for*:

- a. introduces an adverbial of duration;
- b. introduces an adverbial of reason;
- c. introduces an adverbial indicating a beneficiary;
- d. introduces an adverbial indicating a representative;
- e. introduces a noun or adjective complement;
- f. is part of a prepositional verb.

Hint: in looking for adverbials see which question is appropriate.

1. [According to this] modern man has been around **for** 4 hours.
2. Agents know they could face fines of up to £400 **for** breaking the rules...
3. We...will continue to express a world-wide desire **for** peace...
4. Now then what can we do **for** you this time?
5. They will only make a court order if...he's asking **for** the child to go to live with him...
6. ...what was good for a gene might not be good **for** an individual.
7. ...child sponsorship can be harmful **for** the child, her family and community.
8. This is **for** your skin.
9. David Gorman has given science a new slant **for** pupils at Ladymount School...
10. ...he is only the spokesman **for** the work of the thousands of scientists...
11. I'd been sitting there **for** ages...
12. The Awards are valid **for** five years...
13. I've gotta wait **for** a report...
14. Thank you **for** your very kind congratulations...

5.6 *by*

The most common use of *by* is to indicate the agent (or 'doer') in a passive:

> He *was surprised by* the amount of opposition.

It is also possible to say *The amount of opposition surprised him*, where the agent is the subject. This is not to say, of course, that all passives must have a *by* phrase. Indeed, one of the reasons for having a passive is to avoid mentioning the agent.

By can indicate an agent, i.e. the person carrying out an action, even when no passive is involved; the action is represented by a noun: *a statement by the police*. Here, the noun could be turned into a verb: *The police stated…* It can also be used when indicating the creator or author of a work: *a painting by Picasso*.

It is also often used to introduce an adverbial of time, place or manner:

> *By 2005 the numbers had doubled.* (time preceding)
> *I was standing by the building…* ('next to', 'near to')
> *You make matters worse by not answering.* (manner)

Activity 5.6

In the lines below identify where *by* introduces:

  a. an agent following a passive construction
  b. a non-passive agent, as described above
  c. the creator of a work
  d. an adverbial of time, place or manner (and say which).

Hint: for the passive agents try to make them the subject of the clause; for the non-passive agents try to turn the noun into a corresponding verb.

1. The film is rated PG13 in the US, which means children under 13 have to be accompanied **by** an adult.
2. I'm **by** the river bank…I'm featured on the front of a very famous album **by** Pink Floyd.
3. The…court had before it an application **by** the local authority for a care order…
4. On 21 September 1982 Mr. Dennis committed an act of bankruptcy **by** failing to comply with the requirements of a bankruptcy notice.
5. Pioneered **by** Miss Alice Green in 1941, this committee…
6. …more than 40 per cent of arable land…is potentially at risk from erosion **by** wind or water.
7. The JPs…will now be the subject of an inquiry **by** the Lord Chancellor's Office.
8. …the costume must be made **by** the child.
9. …police attacked a candlelit procession **by** about 1,000 young people…
10. He…liked the simplified shapes produced **by** artificial lighting.
11. This material is protected **by** international copyright laws…
12. …gipsy songs **by** Brahms are being performed this evening…
13. Here the judge sought to justify the course he took **by** saying, in effect, that the prosecution case was all but complete.

14. [This] has clearly had a beneficial effect on profits which soared **by** a third…
15. …the class gathers round to look at works **by** Klee, Stanley Spencer, Ingres…

5.7 *at*

At is most commonly used to introduce prepositional phrases functioning as adverbials. These may refer to times:

Here most children start school <u>at five</u>.
The office is closed <u>at weekends</u>.

or to places which are considered to be a point, as opposed to a surface (*on…*) or a container (*in…*):

Where are you now? – I'm <u>at the station</u>.
There were very few people <u>at the book launch</u>.

Such adverbials are questioned using *When…?* or *Where…?*
  At also occurs in prepositional verbs:

Some of them were <u>laughing at</u> me.

Here, the question would be *Who were they laughing at?*, since *at* indicates a prepositional object, not an adverbial.
  There are also some expressions; for example, *at least*.

Activity 5.7

Identify on these lines where *at* introduces an adverbial referring to:

a. time
b. place.

Then try to account for the remaining lines.

Hint: try asking questions with *when* and *where*.

1. Meetings of all tutors are arranged **at** intervals…
2. I write to inform you that the appeal is to be heard **at** the above address…
3. …we lived **at** the top of the second hill and this school was **at** the bottom.
4. …he looked **at** his reflection and found he was a swan.
5. Anne wants it **at** 30 degrees, Pat **at** 60 degrees.
6. Bodelwyddan Castle was the backdrop to a dramatic 'son et lumière' performance **at** the weekend.
7. It takes place **at** the Brighton Community Association…
8. He was Head of the Department of Biological Sciences **at** the University of Dundee between 1968 and 1983…
9. I'm not getting any sleep **at** all.
10. …experts in New Zealand are already calling [it] one of the most remarkable stories ever told of survival **at** sea.

Chapter 6

Adverbs

6.0 Introduction

We have already seen adverbs in Chapter 3, alongside the pronoun and determiner uses of certain words (such as *some* and *much*). We will see another type of adverb – **adverb particles** – in Chapter 9 on multi-word verbs. This chapter deals with the common types of adverb.

As a word class, adverbs are rather problematic, much more so than any other word class, since there is very little that holds them together. Formally, there are a number of endings, such as *-wise* (e.g. *lengthwise*), *-ways* (e.g. *sideways*) and the common *-ly* (e.g. *easily*), but not all such words are adverbs, e.g. *kindly*. Many adverbs have no identifying ending (e.g. *soon*).

Structurally, they are found in the company of many word classes; they may modify almost anything:

- adjectives (<u>*really*</u> *big*)
- other adverbs (<u>*very*</u> *quickly*)
- verbs (*she sang* <u>*quietly*</u>)
- nouns (*the way* <u>*back*</u>)
- clauses (<u>*Fortunately*</u>, *she tested negative*).

Generally they seem to refer to circumstances; that is, to elements in clauses that are less central than nouns and verbs.

Another factor that affects adverbs is their position. They are normally quite moveable, but the default for most is the so-called 'middle position': between the subject and verb, after the first auxiliary if there is one:

Adverbs are <u>usually</u> found in middle position.

A number of different types of adverb can be distinguished:

a. **central adverbs.** These are the words referring to manner, time and place that are traditionally thought of as adverbs and which modify the meaning of the verb or the whole sentence:

She <u>quietly</u> closed the door.

This type of adverb has several possible positions in clauses according to need:

1. The thirty year old is **still** at home.
2. ...a landlord...may **still** be entitled to re-enter peaceably...
3. ...one man is **still** being questioned in connection with the murder...
4. ...day membership payment facilities will **still** entitle you to use all the facilities.
5. He's **still** our friend.
6. ...the speaker has been cancelled but the evening **still** goes forward...
7. **Still**, he does realise that service companies will feel the pinch too...
8. But her heart, she admits, is **still** in Lebanon.
9. He held the rock and stared at it. The boat came nearer, and nearer **still**...
10. the national survey...showed some seventy two percent of businesses were **still** there after eighteen months.
11. And when she was tired, she **still** walked round and round the shops to find the cheapest food.
12. **Still** waters run deep.

6.2 yet

Yet is a very versatile word with a number of different uses. It is used in three main ways:

1. as an aspect adverb, referring to or asking about something uncompleted, e.g.:

   I haven't done it yet.
   Have you done it yet?

Usually there is a negative or question. Unlike other aspect adverbs, it tends to be placed at the end of clauses rather than in the middle position, though this is possible:

   I haven't yet done it.

As with *already*, there is a difference in verb choice between British and American usage; the latter prefers the past tense to the present perfect:

   I didn't do it yet.

2. as a linking adverb to show a contrasting idea:

   The apartment was small; yet it had a certain charm.
   The apartment was small and yet it had a certain charm. (and is the conjunction)

3. as a **conjunction**, similar in meaning to the linking adverb above, but not preceded by a full stop or semi-colon:

   The apartment was small, yet it had a certain charm.

In addition there are a number of less common uses:

- After the verbs *be* and *have* followed by an **infinitive**, meaning something has not happened:

   We have yet to understand the reasons for the riots.

   This is a formal use.

- With **comparatives** and similar words, to emphasise a greater degree of a quality or a larger amount of something, similar in meaning to *even* (see 6.4). It may come before or after an adjective:

  They were old but she was older yet. (or yet alder)
  There are yet more people waiting for an operation.

  This is formal.

- To make a contrast between two **adjectives**:

  The apartment was small yet comfortable.

Activity 6.2

Decide whether *yet* on these lines is:

a. an aspect adverb
b. a linking adverb
c. a conjunction
d. part of *be/have yet to*
e. emphasising a greater degree or larger amount
f. contrasting two adjectives.

Hint: look at the words around *yet*.

1. Incidentally I always do this and **yet** I must reassure you that I'm not a Saga representative…
2. Britain today has a woman Prime Minister and **yet** just over 70 years ago women were not even able to vote.
3. …there's quite a lot of money going into studies but no commitment **yet** as to actually build it.
4. …it has **yet** to see much return from its substantial investment…
5. Zoologists have **yet** to establish the precise mechanisms behind the camel's fuel economy.
6. I believe that this application for a residence order is **yet** another step in this game…
7. We don't know **yet** if she will have to come home.
8. …the exact day they will be out is not known **yet**…
9. Although pricing has not **yet** been decided, it will be kept low to appeal to the mass market.
10. …the low point came with a telephone call from the factory telling of **yet** more problems.
11. I have not discussed that with the others **yet**…
12. You're going to live for a wee while **yet**…
13. Television has quickly become the most powerful medium, **yet** almost all its programme content is imported…
14. **Yet** although often seen as a tough guy, Bob Hoskins has tried to avoid typecasting.
15. Time doesn't define what feminism is supposed to be, **yet** claims to find a schism…

16. [It] has become a model of how to build low-cost housing on a large, **yet** humane scale.
17. **Yet,** the opportunities that can flow from education and training can also be personally liberating.
18. **Yet** the simplicity is telling.
19. The country's farm-workers and labourers make up 17% of the population, **yet** they are ignored by the mass media.
20. The monuments...have survived for specific reasons **yet** they are only the tip of the iceberg of our archaeological inheritance.

6.3 *already*

In its basic meaning, *already* is used to refer to an event, state or action in the past or present that is perhaps unexpected; for example:

> We *already* know that.

Because of its meaning, it tends to be used with the present perfect in British English, while American English tends to use the past tense:

> We've already *done* that. / We already *did* that.

It is usually placed in middle position, before the main verb and after the auxiliary if there is one, but it can come at the end of sentences:

> We know that *already*.

Activity 6.3

On the following lines for *already*, identify the:

  a. tense used
  b. position.

1. ...domestic agricultural production has **already** been subsidised...
2. It has **already** prepared a detailed Regional Report...
3. ...fans who have **already** bought tickets will find they are still valid...
4. His disclosures have **already** caused several deaths...
5. Many law firms have **already** laid off employees...
6. This can cause even more damage to the throat if the lining is **already** damaged.
7. ...negotiations are reportedly **already** under way with several record companies...
8. ...someone's **already** told him.
9. ...every additional vehicle slows down those **already** there...
10. ...the boat was **already** filling up...
11. ...we **already** have several thousand pounds from British donations...
12. We **already** support over 70 children from the families we visit.

6.4 even

Even is used in a number of ways, usually to indicate something surprising:

a. with **noun phrases** and **verb phrases** to indicate something extreme or unexpected:

Even his supporters are turning against him.
He's even painted the kitchen.

This last example is ambiguous. It could mean 'painted, in addition to doing other things to the kitchen', or 'painted the kitchen in addition to other rooms'. In speech, stress will disambiguate; the position of *even* can also help:

He's painted even the kitchen.

b. with **comparative** adjectives and adverbs, to indicate a level of comparison greater than already mentioned or suggested:

She runs even faster than her brother.

c. as part of two **subordinating conjunctions**, *even though* and *even if*, which express a stronger idea of concession or condition than *though* and *if*:

He'll get the job, even though he doesn't deserve it.
Even if you say you didn't do it, they won't believe you.

d. as an **adjective**:

I would say the chances are even that he'll come.

Activity 6.4

Identify whether *even* on these lines is being used:

a. with a noun phrase
b. with a verb phrase
c. before a comparative
d. as part of a conjunction.

Hint: look at the words following *even*.

1. Each pack is divided into 18 sections covering items like stocks and sauces…and **even** herbs and spices.
2. It's not a punishment, but **even** the punishments are not deterring criminals either.
3. However, **even** as blunt an instrument as our questionnaire proved to be a catalyst in providing ideas…
4. **Even** if you did cut one or two admirals, you're not going to make much of a dent…
5. …sometimes accidents do happen, **even** though nobody is really at fault…
6. [They are] equipped with a spoiler at the top of the rear hatch for **even** greater high speed stability.
7. …she has **even** more experience as a traveller…

8. While high level opening windows are fine..., an opening roof vent is **even** more efficient.
9. In some ways this boom is **even** more extraordinary...
10. ...the plunge in sterling could...force the Government to raise interest rates **even** higher.
11. He's **even** arranged for holes to be drilled into the ash to give the sand martins a head start.
12. **Even** some of the old favourites have had a few imaginative additions...

6.5 *only*

As a focussing adverb (see 6.0), *only* can occur with different types of element to say that something is exclusive, that all other possibilities are excluded:

It is for use only in emergencies.

In this it is similar in meaning to *just* (but not so colloquial) or *solely*. In writing it is usually placed next to the element it modifies, as above, but if the meaning is clear it may be placed elsewhere, particularly in middle position:

It has only applied for one course.

However, there is a potential for ambiguity if there is more than one element that could be focussed on:

He only read the book.

Does this mean he didn't do anything else to the book, or that he didn't read anything else? In speech, stress would make it clear.

It can also be used to refer to a small amount or a short period of time:

I only have five pounds.
I only met her last week. (i.e. not before)

It is also frequently used as an **adjective** with the same meaning as *sole*:

Our only hope is that someone will find him.

Two expressions are worthy of note: *if only*, where it acts as a comment adverb to express a wish:

If only I could remember the name.

and *not only...(but) also*, which functions as a double conjunction stressing two things:

Not only did he disappear, he also took the money.

Activity 6.5

On the lines below work out whether *only* is:

a. an adjective

Hint: try replacing it with *sole*.

b. part of an expression
c. then, work out what element adverb *only* is modifying.

Hint: try moving *only* or replacing it with *nothing else*, or *not more than*.

1. [It] remains an oasis of timeless calm **only** a few paces from the crowded pavements of the city centre.
2. The land is to be used for amenity purposes **only** and is not an agricultural holding...
3. The **only** barriers to participation we put in your way are in the 100-metre-hurdle event.
4. ...outsiders will not **only** be able to find what they are looking for but will also be persuaded to explore further.
5. [This] **only** becomes relevant if the threshold test is met.
6. I was away for a week there, I **only** came back on Saturday.
7. [His] **only** fear is that the sky may fall on his head.
8. Other treatment is free **only** for those from countries with reciprocal agreements...
9. ...you've **only** got a wheeze, there's no evidence of an infection...
10. An award is **only** made when there is evidence that an innovation has achieved commercial success.
11. All's well, if **only** the very large and very sticky buds in the tree-tops would burst into leaf.
12. ...the **only** thing about the freezing is sometimes it doesn't work first time.
13. The design isn't the **only** thing that's new.
14. ...a great deal of these patients get better, and **only** very few fall into problems.
15. Malt whisky is distilled twice; and **only** when the spirit reaches a high enough standard is it collected...

6.6 *also*

Also is a focussing adverb (see 6.0) that adds an idea to something already stated:

He is best-known as an actor but he <u>also</u> <u>plays in a group</u>.

Its normal position is middle, i.e. between subject (+ first auxiliary) and verb (see 6.0), as above, but final position is also possible:

...he plays in a group <u>also</u>.

But there may be some ambiguity; it is not always clear what item is being added. For example:

Teeth <u>also</u> need protection.

Does this suggest 'teeth' in addition to something else, or 'protection' as well as something else? In speech, stress and intonation would help.

Occasionally it is used as a linking adverb (see 6.0) with the same idea of addition, being placed at the start of a sentence:

You should be at work by 9. <u>Also</u>, we expect employees to be decently dressed.

But here *also* connects the ideas in the two sentences as a whole, rather than adding an extra idea.

See 6.5 for the use of the expression *not only...but also*.

Activity 6.6

On the following lines for *also*:

a. note any unusual position;
b. identify what is being added to, what the previous sentence probably states.

Hint: try to identify what *also* is focussing on in the sentences.

1. The institute…will **also** arrange tests on volunteers in order to establish safety…
2. This last setting can **also** be manually selected by the driver.
3. There will **also** be about 20 contemporary masks…
4. Our December meeting is open to the men **also**.
5. The following table…**also** demonstrates how male dominated we were 60 years ago.
6. The newer, more reliable tests…are **also** described…
7. However there are **also** implications for provision policies.
8. Ophthalmic, chiropody, and oral services are **also** planned…
9. It **also** produces spirits locally, either directly or through third party arrangements.
10. Hewitt-Jones **also** wrote orchestral music…

6.7 *hopefully*

Hopefully can be both a central adverb, meaning 'in a hopeful manner':

> *They looked <u>hopefully</u> through the window at the sweets.*

or a comment adverb (see 6.0), meaning 'It is hoped that', or 'I am hopeful that':

> *If we wait the rain will <u>hopefully</u> stop.*

Here, the rain will not 'stop in a hopeful manner'. It is the speaker's hope that is being expressed.

Some people still object to the use of *hopefully* as a comment adverb, arguing that it should only be used as a central adverb, but this use is very widespread nowadays, and there is no reason why it should be singled out as there are many other adverbs used similarly, such as *thankfully*.

Activity 6.7

Decide on the lines whether *hopefully* is a:

a. comment adverb
b. central adverb.

Hint: try moving *hopefully* or replacing it with *in a hopeful manner*.

1. …the years in Peru will **hopefully** have given the lie to that belief.
2. **Hopefully** he'll have calmed down a bit!
3. So please stick to the path at this site and **hopefully** nothing else will need to be done.

4. **Hopefully**, our experience will be of use to them.
5. [It] looks **hopefully** to Alpha to rocket it off its $14,000m-a-year launchpad...
6. ...if I come across the same problem a few times I could **hopefully** work on that...
7. that's one thing I 'll be looking at, in the next few months **hopefully**.
8. **Hopefully**, you've brought along some first aid remedies in your kit bag...

6.8 *however*

However can be both a linking adverb, showing a contradiction between two ideas in separate sentences:

> *Studies such as these can only indicate a statistical association, not prove cause and effect.* *However, in recent years the number and diversity of these studies has grown substantially.*

and a degree adverb with adjectives and adverbs:

> *However hard you try, you'll still fail.*

Here, it means 'it doesn't matter how...'.
    As a linking adverb it is not always placed first in the sentence:

> *In recent years, however, the number and diversity of these studies has grown substantially.*

As can be seen from the examples, in writing commas are normally used to show its separate status.
    It can also be used as a central adverb:

> *However you tell it, it doesn't look good.* (= 'regardless of how...')

Activity 6.8

Distinguish the linking and degree adverb functions of *however* on these lines.

Hint: try moving *however*.

Note: where it is a linking adverb, the first idea will be in a previous sentence.

1. I do, **however**, accept the other parts of Mr. Whitaker's argument.
2. No one **however** at the time questioned why it was necessary to do that.
3. I am by no means certain, **however**, he is right...
4. **However**, if your financial circumstances change after divorce, you may be able to get maintenance with the help of a solicitor.
5. [She] finds it difficult to accept him as a man with a different set of strengths and weaknesses, **however** happy he makes her daughter...
6. **However**, it is not just the severely disabled who can benefit from computers.
7. As an image within the action of the play, **however**, it is soon shattered...
8. **However** official records seem to be almost non-existent.
9. **However**, other cases are more complex...
10. The court is not **however** powerless to regulate its own proceedings in this area.

6.9 *clearly*

Like many other words, *clearly* can be both a central adverb, meaning 'in a clear manner':

> *She speaks very clearly.*

and a comment adverb, expressing the speaker's/writer's opinion:

> *This is clearly not in our interests.*

where it means 'it is clear to me'. In this sense it could also be placed at the start:

> *Clearly this is not in our interests.*

Activity 6.9

Decide on these lines whether *clearly* is a:

a. central adverb
b. comment adverb.

Hint: try replacing it with *in a clear manner*.

1. explains **clearly** and simply Historic Scotland's commitment to its customers...
2. ...the period of remand should **clearly** be as short as possible...
3. This would **clearly** be unfair on the defendant...
4. The Survey makes this point very **clearly**...
5. Can you **clearly**...present the copyright and Intellectual Property issues involved...?
6. They make sure fire instructions are **clearly** displayed...
7. ...as such it is **clearly** drawn from his deepest and happiest memories.
8. Shaw's infatuation with the actress...**clearly** found its way into the script...
9. ...this study has **clearly** identified a major problem area...
10. We are now **clearly** in a mature market...

6.10 *perfectly*

Perfectly is usually thought of as a central adverb of manner:

> *The evening ended perfectly.*

but it can also be a degree adverb:

> *They were perfectly horrible to us.*

It has the idea of 'extremely'; there is no idea of 'perfection' in this example. The central adverb can also modify an adjective:

> *The water was perfectly still.*

Activity 6.10

Decide whether *perfectly* on these lines is a:

    a. central adverb

    b. degree adverb.

Hint: try replacing it with similar words such as *completely* or *totally*.

1. I'm **perfectly** aware of the fact that a lot of men are not very good at taking a woman's opinion…
2. …a high level of teamwork, whilst **perfectly** desirable, is not absolutely essential…
3. …they were **perfectly** entitled to claim this…
4. …the mountains…are mirrored **perfectly** in the waters of the loch.
5. But it's **perfectly** natural, isn't it.
6. You don't have to do it **perfectly** round because the earth isn't **perfectly** round.
7. The other day he seemed **perfectly** sound…
8. For a hundred years sound recordists have been claiming how **perfectly** their recordings represented the original.
9. …it's good for the minute that it was granted but it is **perfectly** useless thereafter.
10. …she knew **perfectly** well that this was not true…

6.11 very

Very is perhaps the most frequent degree adverb (see 6.0), used with adjectives and adverbs (and some determiners) to intensify the quality they express:

We are <u>very</u> happy to meet you.

It can also be an adjective meaning 'exact' or 'precise':

That's the <u>very</u> word I was going to use.

Activity 6.11

Decide whether on these lines *very* is:

    a. a degree adjective

    b. an adjective.

Hint: look at the word following *very*.

1. It was all over **very** quickly.
2. I've still got this sore tongue that keeps coming back, **very** badly.
3. Britain is paying a full part at the **very** centre of the European community.
4. The materials are **very** clearly targeted towards a British undergraduate readership…
5. So it's **very** important we get you seen next week…
6. …a book such as this ought to suggest a greater awareness of the **very** issues it is summarising.

7. But you weren't **very** keen on that...
8. Thanks **very** much Doctor, thank you.
9. It was **very** nice, wasn't it?
10. ...[he] encouraged me to get involved...right from the **very** onset.
11. One has only to look at the United States, where they take sex education **very** seriously...
12. Well the letter will arrive **very** shortly...

6.12 too

Too is used in two major ways: as a degree adverb (see 6.0) with adjectives and adverbs, implying an excessive degree:

That's too high for me.

and as a focussing adverb to add something, similar in meaning to *as well*:

We know them too.

but it is usually placed at the end, as above. It can also be equated with *also*, but the position is different:

We also know them.

As a degree adverb it is often followed by an explanatory phrase or clause:

It's too late to apologise.

Activity 6.12

On the following lines distinguish between the use of *too* as a:

a. degree adverb
b. focussing adverb.

Hint: note the position of *too*.

1. She'll need to watch she doesn't take **too** many of them.
2. It will prove essential reading...not just in tropical countries but in other regions of the world **too**.
3. ...there wasn't **too** much doubt about the penalty decision.
4. The fear is that Brightness is now **too** famous and **too** valuable to be set free.
5. We have waited **too** long for our freedom.
6. Your mum thinks that would be great. – I think so **too**.
7. **Too** often it is forgotten that these should be ways of love and concord.
8. Nintendo was able to take over the US market **too**.
9. I'm usually not **too** bad at keeping a grip on myself.
10. I know the feeling only **too** well.

Chapter 7

Verb patterns

7.0 Introduction

Although they are not the most frequent word class (nouns are), grammatically verbs are the most important word class. A number of factors contribute to this: their different forms, the uses and meanings of the tenses and the construction of verb phrases. Another factor, their use as multi-word verbs, is covered in Chapter 9.

The main reason why verbs are important grammatically is that they are the key element in the construction of clauses, since they determine what other elements appear. The focus in this chapter is on the various arrangements that occur with verbs in clauses; this is called 'verb patterns' (or 'verb complementation').

Basically the elements that are determined by the verb are the 'objects' and 'predicatives' (sometimes called complements) that typically follow the verb. (Verbs can also occasionally determine the selection of **subjects** and **adverbials**.)

Objects refer to things and people that are involved in actions denoted by the verb. There are two types of object in standard treatments: 'direct' and 'indirect'. Direct objects denote things that are directly affected or created by an action:

He told the truth.
They built a house.

Subordinate clauses are common as direct objects, especially **that** clauses after certain verbs of saying and thinking; for example *say, tell* (see 7.8), *think, know, feel* (see 7.12):

They say that it's going to snow.
We know that he has been seeing her.

That can be omitted in all such cases.

Indirect objects usually refer to people who benefit from some action or are recipients:

He's paid me.

Usually indirect objects are found together with direct objects, always occurring first:

He's paid me the money.

Both direct and indirect objects can become the subject in passives:

I've been paid.
The money's been paid.

Predicatives (cf. predicative adjectives in Chapter 4) relate to a quality or characteristic that belongs to another element in the clause, either the subject:

She's <u>a teacher</u>.
He feels <u>happy</u>.

or the object:

They appointed <u>her</u> <u>High Court Judge</u>.
The jury found <u>him</u> <u>guilty</u>.

Unlike objects, they do not introduce an additional entity into the clause, and they cannot be turned into the subject of a passive:

<u>She</u> was appointed High Court Judge. (the object has become the subject)
*?High Court Judge was she appointed by them.

Noun phrases and adjectives are common as predicatives, as above. With an object, a (non-finite) clause, e.g. an **infinitive** phrase, may serve as a predicative:

I <u>heard</u> him <u>open the door</u>. ('He opened the door'.)

Noun phrases are questioned using *what* or *who*, as with objects, but adjectives are questioned using *how*:

<u>How</u> does he <u>feel</u>?

There are five basic patterns for verbs according to the presence of objects and predicatives:

1. intransitive, where there is no object or predicative (though there may be one or more **adverbials**, not underlined below):

    She <u>drove</u> home quickly.

2. link, where there is a predicative only:

    She <u>became</u> <u>a mother</u> at forty.

3. monotransitive, where there is only an object:

    He <u>likes</u> <u>chocolate</u>.

4. ditransitive, where there are two objects (indirect followed by direct):

    I <u>wrote</u> <u>them</u> <u>a letter</u>.

5. link transitive, where there is an object and a predicative:

    We <u>made</u> <u>her</u> <u>happy</u>.

As its name implies, it is a combination of the link and (mono)transitive patterns.

Verbs do not change from being monotransitive or ditransitive just because an object has become a subject of a passive. For example, in:

<u>The letter</u> was written by me.

write should still be considered a monotransitive verb. There are other situations where objects have been 'lost', in that they do not follow the verb, but where they should be considered in deciding the verb's pattern:

- relative clauses: *It's the answer that the teacher wanted.* (*want* is monotransitive)
- questions: *What do I know?* (*know* is monotransitive)
- infinitive phrases: *I have a statement to make.* (*make* is monotransitive)

Most common verbs belong to more than one pattern, often with different meanings associated. Therefore, it can be problematic to classify a verb simply as one of the five types above, to say, for example, that *run* is an intransitive verb. The activities below all involve verbs which are used in more than one way.

Knowledge about a verb's patterns can help to explain why certain constructions are incorrect. Thus:

> **I explained her the problem.*

is wrong because *explain* does not occur in the ditransitive pattern (unlike similar verbs such as *tell*). It is necessary to say *I explained the problem to her.*

Reference is made in some of the sections to multi-word verbs (i.e. phrasal and prepositional verbs) since they are common with some of the verbs below. However, such cases are dealt with fully in Chapter 9 and so only limited examples have been included here. A third type of object that some grammars recognise, prepositional objects, is considered in Chapter 9.

Of the three 'primary auxiliaries', *be*, *have* and *do*, only the last two are included since they have more than one pattern as a main verb. *Be*, although it is the most common verb in English, is not very 'interesting' since it occurs in only one pattern (a link verb) in addition to its role as an auxiliary.

The basic form of the verb selected in the lines below serves as the infinitive, present tense and imperative. In the case of **irregular verbs** it may also serve as past tense and *-ed* participle. Such cases will be noted below.

The verbs below are a somewhat random collection, unlike the words in most of the other chapters. They have been chosen to cover all the possible combinations of patterns, and all are common verbs.

7.1 *have*

By far the most common use of *have* is as an auxiliary in the formation of perfect verb phrases:

> *I have lived here for 23 years.*
> *I have been coming here for ages.*
> *They have been cheated.*

It is also frequent as a main verb:

- in a monotransitive pattern:

> *We have many friends around the world.*

Have got is an alternative, especially in British English:

We *have got* many friends around the world.

Technically, *have* is an auxiliary here:

- or in a link transitive pattern, with a bare infinitive phrase as the predicative:

I'll *have* *him* *call you*.

In its monotransitive use it may occur in questions and negatives without **do** support (see 7.2 below), as though it were an auxiliary:

I *haven't* the faintest idea.

Also possible are:

I *don't have* the faintest idea.
I *haven't got* the faintest idea.

Another use of *have* is in the semi-modal *have to* (also *have got to*):

We *have to* be careful how we approach him.

As an alternative to *must*, this use is also discussed in Section 8.9.

Activity 7.1

On the lines below decide whether *have* is being used as:

a. an auxiliary
b. a monotransitive verb
c. a link transitive verb
d. a semi-modal, part of *have to*.

Note: the auxiliary use of *have* is under-represented here.

Hint: check whether *have* is followed by a noun (probably an object) or a verb.

1. ...we do not **have** an organisation in the country that has a monitoring role for the quality...
2. Do you **have** to have braces then?
3. Dogs and sheep **have** died after drinking near blooms.
4. I don't **have** enough to last me four weeks...
5. ...they **have** only themselves to blame.
6. In fact they may recommend they **have** people see him.
7. I must **have** spent a couple of thousand pounds on these photos.
8. We **have** to realise that a significant proportion of our soils are fragile.
9. I'll **have** words with Sharon on Monday...
10. **Have** you got any swollen glands in your neck?

7.2 do

The two main uses of *do* are as a monotransitive verb:

> I promise I'll <u>do</u> it.

and as an auxiliary to provide what is sometimes called **do** support in forming questions and negatives with verbs:

> <u>Do</u> you know him?
> I <u>do</u> not understand the question.

As an auxiliary it is also used to make emphatic statements:

> I <u>do</u> know him.

and invitations:

> <u>Do</u> have a seat.

It can also be used as a:

- ditransitive verb: *Can you <u>do</u> me a drink?*
- intransitive verb: *That will <u>do</u>!* (= 'That's enough!')

Activity 7.2

On the lines below, work out whether *do* is being used:

a. in a monotransitive pattern
b. as an auxiliary.

There is one line where *do* does not fit either category. What is it and why?

Hint: look at the word following *do*.

1. **Do** have a seat, I'm trying to **do** eight things at once as usual.
2. …we want to be able to live on an island, without being told what to **do**…
3. It's quite normal to **do** that…
4. Let's see you actually **do** something for a change.
5. …will you **do** that for me?
6. …the best thing to **do** is for me to tell them…
7. We'll try this for a couple of weeks and see how things **do**.
8. [They] **do** not shy away from controversy.
9. Please **do** not send any money at this stage.
10. What else can I **do** for you?
11. What can we **do** for this young man?
12. **Do** you think it's the drink that's doing that?

7.3 *run*

Run is commonly thought of as an intransitive verb, meaning a fast form of movement:

He was <u>running</u> with a strange rolling movement.

However, it is quite common as a monotransitive verb, meaning 'manage' or 'organise':

She <u>runs</u> a multi-million-dollar business from her back room.

In this, it is often used in the passive:

The company needs to be <u>run</u> more efficiently.

There are other intransitive meanings:

'operate': *Trams <u>run</u> till midnight.*
'last': *The show should <u>run</u> for years.*

In addition, taps 'run' (with water) and colours 'run' (mix when clothes are washed).

Run is common as a phrasal verb; for example, *to run up a bill*. There are some examples on the lines below.

Note that it is an irregular verb and *run* serves as *-ed* participle, as in the passive example above, as well as infinitive, present tense and imperative.

Activity 7.3

Decide whether *run* on the following lines is used as:

a. an intransitive verb
b. a monotransitive verb.

Also identify where the meanings depart from the typical meaning of the physical movement and management/organisation.

Hint: try turning active sentences into the passive.

1. [It] could be **run** on a regular basis.
2. And she began to **run** along the road to him.
3. ...the very next week he was **run** over and killed by a bus...
4. Another aspect of [her] job is to **run** seven audio visual educational libraries...
5. We've got to know the people who **run** the centre...
6. When fermentation has finished the green beer is **run** into conditioning tanks for a few days.
7. ...in 1931 [the line] was closed to passengers but continued to **run** for freight only...
8. At first CAMRA was **run** on a purely voluntary basis...
9. She wanted her baby, did not want to **run** the risk of a miscarriage...
10. [He] has since **run** in several races for the club...
11. [This] makes it illegal to **run** onto the pitch...
12. The measures will **run** to the end of 1990...

13. I used to **run** a training course on how to **run** exhibitions…
14. …we **run** the vending operation for the yard.
15. It's time for me to **run** along…

7.4 set

Set is used as both a monotransitive verb, with one object:

> He _set_ _the vase_ on the window-sill.

or as a ditransitive verb, with two objects:

> I've _set_ _them_ _a quiz_.

> *Set* is also commonly used as a phrasal verb:

> The document _sets out_ new procedures for vetting applicants.

This is dealt with fully in Chapter 9. Some examples are included in the lines below.

Set is an irregular verb. Thus 'set' serves as *-ed* participle and past tense, as well as infinitive, present tense and imperative.

There is also a related adjective, *set*, which is derived from the *-ed* participle. It is often followed by a *to* infinitive:

> The stock is _set_ _to_ gain in value.

Activity 7.4

Decide whether *set* on the following lines is:

a. a monotransitive verb
b. a ditransitive verb
c. an adjective.

Ignore whether it is a phrasal verb.

Hint: try to identify the object noun phrases following the verb by replacing them with a pronoun.

1. This is the basis upon which the English court has **set** aside convictions resting upon identification…
2. …we've **set** aside a room…
3. [He] speaks of him with great admiration and has himself **set** him all the tests…
4. **Set** the bench at an angle of 30°s…
5. I **set** the table but I forgot about the water.
6. Chimes of Freedom and Dead Certain look **set** to dominate the betting.
7. …it was **set** two broad objectives…
8. …every enterprise **set** up has still to pay the penalty of remoteness…

7.5 *make*

Make is a very frequent verb, used in a number of different patterns with differing meanings. It can be:

- monotransitive:

  Don't *make* a fuss.

- link transitive:

  You *make* me sick.

  This includes cases where the predicative is a bare infinitive:

  We'll *make* them *pay*.

- ditransitive:

  I'll *make* him a nice supper.

(cf. I'll make a nice supper for him.)

Activity 7.5

Distinguish between the following patterns for *make* on the lines below:

- a. monotransitive
- b. link transitive
- c. ditransitive.

Hint: try making the noun phrases into the subjects of passives.

1. ...to **make** it easier for you we could meet in Middlesbrough...
2. ...he/she should **make** no attempt to bluff...
3. [They] would do what they could to **make** mischief about it.
4. Is that down to us or should we notify the division to **make** contact?
5. It'll **make** you cough probably...
6. ...did they **make** any difference at all?
7. ...the new...Body is likely to **make** teaching markedly better paid...
8. I don't think stress would cause this sort of pain but it'll certainly **make** it feel worse...
9. It won't **make** me a better player, added Strachan...
10. ...so I commanded her to **make** me a pot of coffee.
11. What we need to do now is **make** them look interesting...
12. ...we'll **make** the appointment when we've got the tablets...
13. Borrowing had to be curbed, and the only way was to **make** it more expensive.
14. Another rise in interest rates would **make** recession much more likely...
15. Do you have to **make** so much noise?
16. ...he added that he would have no announcement to **make** about that in his key speech...
17. What do they **make** at this place?
18. ...what we try to do is to **make** that work more available to the public...

7.6 get

Get is a very versatile verb. It can occur in the following patterns:

- monotransitive, meaning 'fetch' or 'receive':

  I'll go and get the car.
  We get less mail every week.

- link, meaning 'become':

  I'm starting to get sleepy.

- link transitive:

  Why do you always get it wrong?

  especially with an *-ed* participle as predicative:

  Let's get it done quickly.

- ditransitive:

  Can I get you something?

Activity 7.6

On the following lines distinguish between these patterns for *get*:

  a. link
  b. monotransitive
  c. link transitive.

Hint: what follows *get*?

  1. Right, as you can imagine things might **get** a little bit nasty…
  2. I seem to **get** an awful lot of…dry flaky skin.
  3. It is easy to **get** thrown by a detail or a minority comment…
  4. Fiction: You can't **get** burned if you're in the water.
  5. People were comfortable and I could always go and **get** something I wanted.
  6. The reality is that workers at Dagenham can **get** jobs elsewhere…
  7. Don't let the photographer **get** all the perks.
  8. I'll **get** that organized.
  9. Inevitably they do not always **get** it right.
  10. You better go and **get** some tea…
  11. Let's **get** that sorted for you.
  12. …as we **get** wealthier, we want to consume more manufactured goods…

7.7 give

Give is a classic example of a verb that can be both monotransitive:

> They *give* lots of money.

and ditransitive:

> Can you *give* me some advice?

> *Give* is also common in phrasal verbs: *give up, give in, give out*:

> I'll *give out* the assignment next week.

Such examples are not shown below.

Activity 7.7

Work out whether *give* on the lines below is a:

a. monotransitive verb
b. ditransitive verb.

One line does not fit either of these patterns. Which is it and why?

1. The figures **give** an idea of the industries that are most geared towards exporting.
2. Here are some examples which **give** an indication of the variety of structures which can be listed.
3. ...if you **give** him a huge pay rise all he becomes is a rich sinner...
4. **Give** him time, sir. He's not nineteen yet, he'll learn.
5. [They] were urged not to **give** if they were in risk categories.
6. So you've got to **give** it some heat to help the oxygen to work.
7. ...get him to **give** me a cheque...
8. Unfortunately, however, he could **give** no indication of an average contract value...
9. I believe if we make an effort we can **give** people food.
10. ...he used to go and **give** speeches in the barn.
11. How much time do I need to **give**?
12. I'll just **give** these folks coming in the door a moment...
13. Shortie'll **give** us some money for petrol...
14. We'll **give** you a full report on what we're supplying.
15. I'm certainly not going to **give** you something you don't want...

7.8 tell

Tell can be a:

- monotransitive verb, usually with a direct object:

> All pictures *tell* a story.
> I can *tell* that you're not happy.

but sometimes with an indirect object:

You can tell me.

- ditransitive verb:

Tell us the news.

especially when the direct object is a subordinate clause:

He's trying to tell us that he's not coming.
I can't tell you how thrilled I am.

or a non-finite clause:

They tell us to be careful.

It can also be an intransitive verb in the sense of 'decide':

Only time will tell.

Activity 7.8

Decide whether *tell* on the lines below is:

  a. ditransitive
  b. monotransitive.

On one of the lines, *tell* is neither monotransitive or ditransitive. Which is it?

Hint: try replacing noun phrases or clauses with *this* or *it*.

  1. So I mean that day we had to **tell** a lot of lies, you know…
  2. …one of the reasons I would never wear one is…you can always **tell**…
  3. Oh what grand stories she did **tell**.
  4. They **tell** each other stories…
  5. Now if you see her, **tell** her how much we missed her.
  6. …the family had to come and **tell** him where the grave was.
  7. Now **tell** me what you've got, one at a time…
  8. Every time they **tell** me, they started laughing.
  9. Okay, you **tell** me why you're here.
 10. The new guidelines will **tell** the police to give no more than two cautions…
 11. We'll speak to them and **tell** them that we know what 's happened to you.
 12. I **tell** them everything I've been doing.
 13. And whether that price is worth paying is something only you can **tell** us.
 14. I always **tell** you the truth, you know that.
 15. It's what they don't **tell** you that's important.

7.9 *ask*

Ask is used as a monotransitive verb, either with an indirect object:

You'd better <u>ask</u> <u>him</u>.

or with a direct object:

Can I <u>ask</u> <u>something</u>?

It is also a ditransitive verb:

I wanted to <u>ask</u> you a question.

Subordinate and non-finite clauses are common as direct objects:

Don't <u>ask</u> me <u>why I did it</u>.
I'll <u>ask</u> her <u>to come</u>.

Ask is very common in the prepositional verb *ask for* (see Chapter 9).

Activity 7.9

On the lines below identify where *ask* is:

a. monotransitive, and whether the object is direct or indirect
b. ditransitive
c. part of *ask for*.

Hint: try replacing noun phrases with questions beginning *Who...* (for indirect objects) and *What...* (for direct objects).

1. **Ask** a trusted family member to babysit your children...
2. **Ask** at the Box Office for membership details the next time you are in town.
3. That being so, one must **ask** at what level of readership the book is directed.
4. ...we **ask** for nominations to fill the three places on the Executive Committee...
5. ...she was going to **ask** her boss for a transfer...
6. So you'd have to **ask** him...
7. ...we just have to **ask** how many of our congregation have been added during that time?
8. That's the sort of question to **ask** Stevie...
9. We will **ask** the local people to participate in the project...
10. I'll actually approach and **ask** them to put it out.
11. Ah, I was just gonna **ask** you that.
12. ...I've got to **ask** you to have a look at it...

7.10 *close*

Close can be both intransitive:

Businesses have had to <u>close</u> because of the protests.

and monotransitive:

>*They have had to <u>close</u> their businesses because of the protests.*

However, in this respect it is unlike other verbs which are both intransitive and monotransitive, where the subject stays the same:

>*<u>I</u> drive to work.*
>*<u>I</u> drive my car to work.*

With *close* it is the object of the monotransitive verb (*businesses* in the above examples) which 'becomes' the subject in the intransitive pattern. This pattern is sometimes called 'ergative', to distinguish it from the normal intransitive/monotransitive pattern.

The ergative pattern also applies to the phrasal verb *close down* (see Chapter 9), which can also be both intransitive and monotransitive in the same way.

Activity 7.10

On the lines below distinguish between the use of *close* as:

a. an intransitive verb
b. a monotransitive verb.

Hint: is there an object following the verb?

1. County councillors confirmed this week that the homes will **close**…
2. …we're afraid the scheme will have to **close** down.
3. …schools will **close** for the rest of the week.
4. The colliery is to **close** in just over two weeks' time.
5. …the Society has reluctantly decided to **close** its list to applicants…
6. I **close** the curtains against the night…
7. So it was considered…that the best solution would be to **close** the school for the afternoon.
8. So **close** your eyes.

7.11 *grow*

Grow is typically used in three patterns:

- as an intransitive verb:

>*This plant will <u>grow</u> only in humid conditions.*

As in the example there is often an adverbial following (not to be confused with an object).

- as a link verb meaning 'become':

>*As we <u>grow</u> older, our memory starts to fade.*

- as a monotransitive verb:

>*I've never tried to <u>grow</u> my own potatoes.*

It is also frequent in the phrasal verb (see Chapter 9) *grow up*:

> You'll never <u>grow up</u> if you eat all those sweets.

Activity 7.11

On the lines below work out whether *grow* is used as:

a. an intransitive verb
b. a monotransitive verb
c. a link verb.

Hint: what follows the verb?

1. Around the fort would **grow** a tiny settlement...
2. ...we would not have been able to **grow** as successfully as we have without it.
3. I learned that my soil was too heavy to **grow** decent carrots or beetroot...
4. ...I can't say I suffered anything having let my brain **grow** dull.
5. ...you can **grow** human skin in a cell culture...
6. ...one that assumes that dividends will **grow** in the future at a constant annual rate...
7. ...we **grow** more concerned and more aware of our environment...
8. Most of us, as we **grow** older, become explorers of the past.
9. Crops **grow** quickly once the weather improves.
10. Their slopes **grow** some of the finest tea in the world.
11. We still **grow** some of the varieties listed a hundred years ago...
12. The secret which I now divulge is that they are dead easy to **grow**.

7.12 *feel*

Feel can occur in a link pattern, followed by an adjective referring to one's condition:

> We're <u>feeling happier</u> now that he's got a job.

or in a monotransitive pattern, either with a noun phrase as object denoting a sensation:

> He suddenly <u>felt a cold wind</u>.

or with a **that** clause indicating an opinion:

> I <u>feel that she hasn't reached her full potential</u>.

Activity 7.12

On the following lines work out whether *feel* occurs in a:

a. link pattern
b. monotransitive pattern.

Hint: try asking a question beginning with *How* or *What* (*do you feel?*)

1. I **feel** appalled by the way these professional guardians have treated us.
2. I **feel** better than I was…
3. …apart from that he **feels** fine, he doesn't **feel** ill…
4. …you **feel** it's a shame to be seen holding on.
5. But he washed his face with cold water, and he began to **feel** much better…
6. He knows how to argue, and perhaps you will **feel** sorry for him…
7. I **feel** strongly that this consensus is our strength.
8. I **feel** such an enormous amount of emotion in all three pieces.
9. …readers of a journal like this may well **feel** that this book does not go far enough.
10. …if you **feel** that the pains are bad during the night, take them at bedtime.
11. They can come to **feel** they are failures.
12. [The] students have made us **feel** very welcome.

Chapter 8

Modal auxiliaries

8.0 Introduction

The modal auxiliaries comprise nine words: *can, could, may, might, shall, should, will, would* and *must*. All of them are considered below.

They are sometimes called **modal verbs**, but here they are treated as a separate word class, distinct from verbs, because:

- unlike verbs, they constitute a **closed word class**;
- their grammar is very different from that of verbs;
- the meanings they refer to are to do with the idea of modality (see below).

Unlike verbs, modals are limited to only one form. They are sometimes called 'defective' verbs because they have:

- no infinitive form (**To can or not to can?*)
- no third-person -s present tense (**she cans*)
- no past tense (**I canned*; see below)
- no -ed or -ing participles (* *I have canned*, **I am canning*).

Structurally they form the first part of **verb phrases**:

   I <u>should</u> go.

although there may be other **auxiliaries** following:

   I <u>would</u> <u>have been</u> laughing by now.

and only one modal is allowed:

   *We <u>must</u> <u>can</u> help you.

Traditionally they have been arranged into four pairs containing 'present' and 'past' forms:

   can/could, may/might, shall/should, will/would (with the status of *must* unclear).

However, while there is a historical basis for this, there is no justification in modern usage. The relationship between, say, *may* and *might* is definitely not the same as that between *see* and *saw*; for one thing both *may* and *might* can refer to the future:

We may come./We might come.

Many of the meanings of one have no parallel in the partner (see below).

Although their forms are simple, the meanings of modals are difficult to account for. There are many, sometimes overlapping, meanings. In the most general terms they all have the idea of **modality**: drawing back from a factual statement to limit the meaning of verbs, similar to the way determiners affect nouns. Thus:

I like him.

is presented as a fact, while:

I should/may like him.

is not.

This involves them in pragmatic factors such as tentativity, commitment (to a proposition), politeness and formality. Thus:

Could you tell me the time?

is not a question about ability, but rather a polite way of making a request for information.

One basic meaning distinction can be made about modals: the difference between 'intrinsic' and 'extrinsic' meanings. (There are other terms used to describe this.) Intrinsic modality refers to the speaker's attempts to control and influence events, and involves meanings such as permission, obligation, intention and promise. Extrinsic modality refers to the way people perceive events as possible, necessary or likely. For example:

You may go. (intrinsic, permission – 'I give you permission to leave')
They may leave. (extrinsic, possibility – 'Their leaving is possible – this is what I think')

These two types of meaning affect all the modals; details are given in the sections below.

All the modals (apart from *can*) can occur with a 'perfect infinitive', i.e. are followed by *have* plus an **-ed participle**, for example:

We could have had it all.

These generally supply reference to past time that is sometimes lacking from the use of modals with a simple infinitive (*We could have it all.*). Details are given in the sections below.

The modals are often grouped with other words:

- the 'marginal modals' *need* and *dare* because of their occasional use as modals (they are dealt with in 8.10);
- the so-called 'semi-modals' (e.g. *have to, ought to, be able to, used to, be going to*), because of their similar meanings, and the ability of the latter to replace the modals in certain situations; for example:

We must go./We have to go.

These cases are dealt with below in the individual sections.

8.1 *can*

Can has three main meanings:

1. to indicate that something is a general possibility (an extrinsic meaning):

    You can get sunburnt even through clouds.

    It can be paraphrased using 'it is possible':

    It is possible for you to get sunburnt...

    In this meaning it often has the idea of something happening occasionally:

    It can snow here in winter. (= 'it snows sometimes')

    It is not used for specific possibilities:

    *It can rain tonight.

    Here, *could, may* and *might* can be used instead.

2. to give permission (an intrinsic meaning):

    You can go out but you must be back by midnight.

    It can be paraphrased with 'be allowed to':

    You are allowed to go out... or I give you permission...

3. to indicate ability:

    I can't swim.

    Here, *can* can be paraphrased with 'be able to' (*I'm not able to swim*). It is commonly used with verbs of perception (where other languages would not use its equivalent):

    I can see what she's pointing to. (?I see what...)

Compared to *can*, *may* is a more formal way of referring to possibility or permission (but not ability):

You may get sunburnt even through clouds.
You may go out but you must be back by midnight.

Can can be ambiguous; it is not always clear which of these three meanings applies:

You can wear anything.

Here, it is not clear whether the speaker is giving permission or is referring to the listener's ability (*Lucky you, you can wear anything*).

Can is also used to make offers:

Can I get you something?

and in requests for action or information:

Can you pass me the remote?

Here, though ostensibly this is a **yes/no question** about the listener's ability, it would not be appropriate to answer *yes* or *no* (and do nothing), because in fact this is an indirect request for action, more polite than saying *Pass me the remote*.

Activity 8.1

Decide on the following lines whether *can*:

a. refers to a possibility
b. refers to permission
c. refers to an ability
d. introduces a request.

Hint: try replacing *can* with *be possible that*, *be able (to)* or *be allowed to*.

1. Phosphates **can** also be released into lakes and rivers from industrial waste...
2. This year, that concern **can** be put into words by everyone who takes part.
3. ...we'll get an appointment out to you as quick as we **can**.
4. Good idea but extensions **can** cause heating problems.
5. ...we guarantee it, so you **can** choose in confidence.
6. ...this work **can** easily be done by any office worker...
7. You **can** help by joining the Research Defence Society and supporting our work...
8. ...excuse me, **can** I ask a question?
9. **Can** I have a signing off form for the insurance please?
10. What **can** I do for you today?
11. Lifts **can** often be arranged or you can make your own way.
12. These bacteria **can** produce powerful and dangerous toxins.
13. ...cars **can** run on unleaded fuel.

8.2 *could*

The meanings of *could* are similar to those of *can*. They indicate:

- possibility: *We <u>could</u> have driverless cars in ten years' time.*
- ability: *I <u>could</u> help you with your homework.*
- permission (rare): *<u>Could</u> I leave now?*
- requests: *<u>Could</u> you give me a hand?*

Could generally refers to present and especially future time, so in no way can it be regarded as the past of *can*. In fact, the two are interchangeable in many situations:

> *I <u>could/can</u> help you with your homework.*

The main difference seems to be that *could* is more tentative than *can*.

However, in some circumstance *could* does refer to past time; for example, with long-term abilities in the past:

> *When I was young I <u>could</u> speak French.*

This is not possible with short-term abilities:

*Yesterday, I _could_ go to work.

unless it occurs with **verbs of perception**:

When I opened the door I _could_ hear nothing.

or in **reported speech**:

He asked if there was somewhere they _could_ talk in private.

But there is no restriction on _could not_ referring to the past:

Yesterday, I _couldn't_ go to work.

In situations where _could_ cannot be used to refer to a past ability, the semi-modal _be able to_ can be used:

You _were able to_ go to work yesterday.

This implies that the action took place. To imply that it did not, _could have_ followed by an -ed participle can be used:

You _could have gone_ to work yesterday.

Could have can also be used for past possibilities:

It _could have rained_ last night.

Activity 8.2

Decide on the following lines whether _could_:

a. refers to possibility, and whether the time is present or future
b. refers to ability, and whether the time is past or future
c. introduces a request.

Hint: try paraphrasing with _be able to_ to distinguish between ability and possibility.

1. Patients on life-saving drugs **could** be taking ineffective or dangerous counterfeit products...
2. ...he hopes the two issues **could** be resolved then.
3. ...owners **could** be liable to the same punishment.
4. It **could** become a money spinner for farmers looking for alternative crops...
5. ...there was nothing more he **could** do to save [it] from crashing...
6. P drivers **could** even be limited to low speeds.
7. I'd just like to ask if we **could** have a meeting about the future of the gallery.
8. Now **could** I have some cramp tablets, Doctor?
9. If we **could** identify the factors that cause this, it would be possible to interfere...
10. But I think I **could** live with that.
11. Now I **couldn't** quite remember.
12. ...it gave a big boost, which salt or sugar alone **could** not provide.

13. They said 78 per cent **could** now read the bottom line of an optician's sight test card...
14. ...their colleagues' work **could** provide the missing pieces in the puzzle.
15. ...in many ways it **could** serve as a useful introduction to that volume.

8.3 *may*

May has the same distinction between intrinsic permission and extrinsic possibility as *can*:

> You *may* begin the exam. (permission, intrinsic)
> It *may* rain. (possibility, extrinsic)

However, it is more formal than *can*, especially for permission. Unlike *can*, *may* is not used for ability.

It may be ambiguous:

> They *may* not use the internet.

This could mean 'they are not allowed to...' or ' they possibly do not...', but the context will normally disambiguate.

May does not refer to past time. To refer to a past possibility *may have* followed by an *-ed* participle can be used:

> She *may have forgotten* the time of the meeting.

Activity 8.3

Decide whether *may* on the following lines refers to:

a. possibility
b. permission.

Hint: try paraphrasing *may* with 'be possible' or 'be allowed to'.

1. ...tutors **may** also be invited to conduct Tutorial Classes...
2. ...a rumour surfaced here yesterday morning that another cut **may** be coming.
3. ...she **may** be unduly pessimistic about that...
4. ...we **may** expect special issue stamps to become even more gimmicky...
5. We **may** finish today but I don't think so.
6. I **may** have my own ideas...
7. ...we **may** have to reduce short run output.
8. ...you **may** have heard of the famous state of the union address to congress...
9. ...if you go to a medical practice you **may** have four or five doctors to help you out.
10. This material is protected by international copyright laws and **may** not be copied or redistributed in any way.
11. Because he is grey he **may** not be easy to spot...
12. It **may** not be enough to save them.
13. ...system users **may** not have access to archive material but **may** read copies of it...
14. ...school management **may** well suspect a high level of condoned truancy...
15. ...this **may** yet be [his] most creative period.

8.4 *might*

Might has the same meanings as *may*: to indicate possibility (extrinsic) or permission (intrinsic). When referring to possibility it is more tentative than *may*, suggesting the speaker considers it less likely:

> It *might* rain (but don't hold your breath).

It is rarely used to indicate permission:

> You *might* leave early today.

This could only be interpreted as possibility, However, it is possible in questions:

> *Might* we leave now?

and in reported speech:

> The boss said we *might* leave early today.

It only refers to present and future time, so cannot be regarded as the past of *may*. When followed by *have* and an *-ed* participle, it can imply that something was a possibility but did not happen:

> You *might* *have warned* me. (*Why didn't you?*)

whereas *may have* leaves the possibility open that something happened:

> She *may* *have warned me* but I forgot.

Activity 8.4

Analyse the following lines to see the balance between the two meanings of *might*.

1. …you brake and somebody behind **might** be too close behind you.
2. …the consequences of doing that **might** be enormous.
3. …we **might** be able to make a guess at how old it is.
4. On a dry pitch [he] **might** have gone for goal instead of squaring the ball…
5. It was the sort of contribution to British life which **might** have brought him an honour.
6. I have some leaflets which **might** help you…
7. However, they conceded that this **might** prove expensive…
8. After the match he was asked what punishment he thought he **might** receive.
9. They **might** run off and take it with them.
10. It **might** take months, it **might** take years, it **might** never even be possible.

8.5 *will*

Will is very frequently used to talk about future time and as a result it is sometimes said that it forms the 'future tense' in English. However, there are several arguments against this:

- Tense in English is a matter of morphology, not of structure; i.e. to form the past we add endings (*looked*) rather than placing a separate word in front of the verb. (We would need to say *I look'll* to make it a tense.)

- *Will* does not always refer to future time:

  That will be the postman.

- When it does refer to the future it always has a tinge of another meaning: prediction, promise, etc. (see below).
- Other forms refer more exclusively to future time, e.g. *going to*.
- *Will* belongs grammatically with the modals, as this chapter has shown.

For all these reasons most grammarians say that English has no future tense – just a number of ways of expressing future time.

Will has the same distinction as other modals between intrinsic meanings ('volition') and extrinsic meanings (confidence about a state or action). By volition we mean willingness or commitment to the undertaking of actions:

I will look after the cat. (a promise)
I will take you to court. (a threat)
Will you give me a lift? (a request)
You will do as I say. (an order)

Compare this with extrinsic meanings, indicating confidence about something:

It will rain tonight. (a prediction)
They will be discussing our case right now. (a deduction)

However, the distinction is not always clear:

You will try your best.

This could be an order, especially if *will* is stressed, or a prediction (*You will try your best, I know.*).

Will is sometimes used in the so-called 'first conditional'; that is, a sentence with *if*, to indicate a real possibility:

If you ask nicely, she will say 'yes'.

For more on the so-called conditionals see 8.6.

Will have followed by an *-ed* participle can be used to make a prediction about something in the past:

They will have finished well ahead of time.

Activity 8.5

On the following lines work out whether *will* refers to:

a. future or present time
b. intrinsic or extrinsic meanings.

Hint:

out the meaning: promise/threat/order vs prediction.

1. Once you have registered for the programme you **will** be invited to the induction day...
2. Hannah Vincent, a young playwright, **will** write a play based on the group's workshops...
3. Her initial task **will** be to try and regularise for us all the amount of information...
4. If you don't change your password...then you **will** be excluded from the network.
5. Here blood tests **will** confirm the type of the infection and determine the treatment.
6. If there is an efficient and profitable way of doing business, we **will** find it.
7. Its boss...now fears that some of his 71staff **will** have to be let go.
8. Helping pupils to make informed choices about healthy living **will** influence not only their own future lives but those of their families.
9. ...it is not necessarily a process which in the long term **will** lead to a reasonable balance of land use.
10. There you **will** learn to play hockey or rugby.
11. ...drinkers the world over **will** recognise and be able to enjoy their favourite blend.
12. As you **will** see from the enclosed letter, it would be good if...
13. ...anyone who wants to understand the way the British establishment thought...**will** still learn from him.
14. The Government, however, is likely to press ahead with legislation this autumn which **will** tighten up the law on secondary action.
15. **Will** we ever learn?

8.6 *would*

Would was sometimes said to form the 'conditional tense' in English. This is no longer tenable, in the same way that *will* cannot be called the 'future tense'; see 8.5).

Nevertheless, there is no doubt that *would* is frequently associated with the idea of conditions, either implicitly (where the condition is not stated), or explicitly in sentences where the condition is expressed using *if*. This has led to the establishment in pedagogic grammars of a number of formulaic sentences: the so-called 'first, second and third conditionals', which have *if* in the **subordinate clause**, and *will* (see 8.5) or *would* in the **main clause**:

> *If I was in charge I would do something about it.* (second conditional)
> *If I had been in charge I would have done something about it.* (third conditional)

In fact, however, there are many other possible combinations of verb forms, and all modals can be used in conditionals:

> *If I had been in charge I could have done something about it.*

Often the condition itself is not explicitly mentioned, only the potential outcome:

> *We would be delighted.* (*to be invited*)
> *I would apologise.* (*if I were you*)

Would is used in a number of other ways:

- to refer to an action that implies future time starting from a point in the past:

They knew they <u>would</u> be unsuccessful. (and they were unsuccessful)

and similarly in **reported speech**:

She said she <u>would</u> attend.

- to make tentative comments about the present and future:

I <u>would</u> recommend we postpone a decision.
I <u>would</u> agree with you.
<u>Would</u> you mind leaving the door open? (a request)

Would like is common in this respect to express a wish:

I <u>would like</u> to say how grateful I am.

- to talk about past habits:

Every Friday we <u>would</u> go down to the disco.

In this it is similar to the semi-modal *used to* (*Every Friday we <u>used to</u>...*).

The intrinsic/extrinsic distinction is not so important to *would* because of its involvement with conditions, which may reflect either meaning.

Activity 8.6

Decide whether *would* on these lines refers to:

    a. an explicit conditional, using *if* (and which exemplify the second conditional)
    b. an implicit conditional, where there is no clause using *if*
    c. future in the past (including reported speech)
    d. past habits
    e. a tentative statement.

Hint: try to work out the meaning, in particular whether the action of the main verb took/ takes place.

    1. ...it **would** be helpful if you actually did fill in that before you actually left...
    2. [He] said again in a BBC interview there **would** be no unilateral cease-fire...
    3. ...they had checked twice before booking that there **would** be no smokers on their coach...
    4. If anyone **would** like to come along some Thursday evening and share something with us we **would** be delighted to hear from you.
    5. [This] **would** cause a global sea-level rise of 4 to 6mm per year.
    6. [The] Council says a new church...**would** create parking problems...
    7. If she put as much energy into her work as into her play, she **would** do much better...
    8. What type of work did they do? – Well...they **would** help to lift potatoes and they **would** stack corn and hay.

9. Mozart **would** not have survived the treatment.
10. If our concentration is going to be on testing, then that **would** not be welcome.
11. ...to overhaul a waggon it **would** probably take you, probably a week.
12. ...he believed it **would** require a public stake to complete the project.
13. ...if we are to take on a proper campaigning role as Oxfam has done, then this **would** require additional staff with the necessary experience...
14. I **would** suggest that this should be payable once a year...
15. ...they might not want to go on national television and say that, which I **would** sympathize with entirely...

8.7 shall

Shall is by far the least frequent of the modal auxiliaries. Like *will*, it has a general meaning of futurity, but as with *will*, there is an added element of meaning, either prediction (an extrinsic meaning):

> When <u>shall</u> we meet again?

or commitment to a proposition to indicate the resolve of the speaker(s) or a promise made (an intrinsic meaning):

> We <u>shall</u> never surrender.

The subject of the verb phrase tends to be *we* or *I*.

The intrinsic meaning of promise is common in formal academic writing to make a metatextual comment:

> We <u>shall</u> return to this in the next chapter.

Here, *will* is possible but sounds less formal.

Shall is also common in formal legal language, such as in contracts and laws, to indicate authority:

> If a committal order is made, the order <u>shall</u> be for the issue of a warrant of committal...

Will is not possible here, without losing the force of the statement.

Another use of *shall* is in suggestions:

> <u>Shall</u> we stay in tonight?

Will is not possible here in standard English.

Some old grammars of English give a paradigm for the 'future tense' in English where *shall* is given the role of a suppletive form of *will* used with first person pronouns (*I* and *we*), while *will* occurs in the second and third **person**. We saw in 8.5 that there is no case for positing a future tense in English; the likelihood of *shall* occurring with first person pronouns is merely a reflection of its involvement with personal commitment. Beyond this we have seen frequent cases where *will* is used with first person (see 8.5) and where *shall* is used with other persons (see above).

Shall followed by *have* and an *-ed* participle indicates a past time from a point in the future:

> I <u>shall have built</u> a new life for myself by then.

This functions as a prediction.

Activity 8.7

On the following lines, decide where *shall* could be replaced by *will* without changing the meaning (apart from perhaps a lessening in formality). On the lines where replacement could not take place, explain why.

1. I **shall** also write to the Captain for addresses…
2. …the minimum price which may be paid for a Share **shall** be 25p…
3. If you don't give me your car insurance details, I **shall** call the police!
4. In this section, we will use weighting factors, whereas in the next section we **shall** describe a different…approach.
5. In this section we **shall** have a brief look at the latter method.
6. Well, I'll see you in the office tomorrow morning, **shall** I?
7. **Shall** I give her a ring and ask her to fax it?
8. I'm absolutely confident…that we **shall** raise our targets.
9. In advance of the seminar we **shall** send a copy of the interim report to all those attending.
10. It means we shall still be among our friends…
11. I **shall** talk about a breakaway fragment in order to emphasize my point.
12. **Shall** we defer this to the General Purposes Committee meeting?

8.8 *should*

Should has the same distinction as other modal auxiliaries between an extrinsic meaning, indicating strong probability:

> That *should* do the trick.

and an intrinsic one, indicating light obligation:

> You *shouldn't* believe everything they tell you.

In this there is less force than *must*.

The semi-modal *ought to* can replace *should* for both these meanings:

> That *ought to* do the trick.
> You *oughn't to* believe everything they tell you.

Should can also serve:

- as a formal alternative to *would* in making requests after *I* and *we*:

> I *should* be grateful if you would telephone me immediately.

There is no suggestion here of necessity or obligation. Note how changing the pronoun changes the meaning to obligation: You *should* be grateful…

- as a less formal alternative to the mandative **subjunctive**:

> We demand that he *should* be disciplined. (cf. …that he be disciplined.)

- in cases of inversion to indicate a formal conditional sentence:

Should you have any questions, do not hesitate to ask. (= 'If you should…')

Ought to is not possible here.

Should have plus an *-ed* participle can refer to things that 'wrongly' did not happen:

You *should have been* here earlier.

Activity 8.8

Work out whether *should* on the following lines:

    a. indicates a light form of obligation in the present or future
    b. indicates strong probability
    c. introduces a formal request
    d. refers to a past obligation which did not happen.

Hint: Try to identify obligation by replacing *should* with *needs to* (though the meaning changes slightly).

1. …the judge **should** allow the matter to be tried by the jury.
2. The system **should** allow the system manager to remove users from the system…
3. …newest editions **should** be available from any public reference library.
4. I **should** be obliged if you would now take the appropriate steps…
5. The VDU image **should** be capable of identifying the structure of the text.
6. The package itself **should** be carefully examined for change during storage…
7. Changes in the container…**should** be looked for and reported.
8. …if our relationship means anything, we **should** be honest.
9. Both cases raise the question of just how the press **should** cover this type of crime.
10. …we believe food **should** do you good as well as taste good.
11. This change **should** enable many members to obtain a discount…
12. …it is an extremely significant claim which **should** have been made explicitly…
13. That **should** have prompted the police to question him closely, but they never did.
14. Without democracy we wouldn't be able to say who **should** rule…

8.9 *must*

As with other modals, the distinction between intrinsic and extrinsic applies to *must*. Intrinsically it indicates a strong obligation:

I *must* go.

In this it can be considered to have more force than *should* (see 8.8):

I *should* go.

Extrinsically it indicates a deduction, i.e. working something out based on evidence:

That *must* be the postman. (on hearing some noise outside)

Compared to *will* (see 8.5), it suggests greater certainty:

That will be the postman.

It can also indicate that something is considered to be necessary.

It must rain soon.

The two meanings can sometimes be hard to distinguish. The following well-known comment is intentionally ambiguous:

You must be crazy to work here.

It could mean: 'it is necessary to be crazy to work here' or 'because you are working here I deduce that you are crazy'.

Must does not refer to past time, only to present and future. To indicate a past obligation a suitable form of the semi-modal *have to* can be used:

I'm sorry, I had to do it.

Have to can also be used to make it clear that an obligation does not exist at present but in the future:

You will have to do it.

When used in the negative, *must* and *have to* convey very different meanings:

I must not do it.

means an obligation not to do something, whereas:

I do not have to do it.

means an absence of obligation.

Must have followed by an *-ed* participle can only refer to a deduction about the past, not to obligation:

I must have done it.

Compare this with *I had to do it.*

Activity 8.9

Decide whether *must* on the following lines indicates:

    a. obligation
    b. deduction
    c. necessity.

Hint: try to paraphrase with *be obliged to, will* (but stronger), or *it is necessary that.*

    1. I would be very keen to do it, I **must** admit.
    2. But you **must** agree that it all looks very strange.
    3. I **must** ask you to think again.
    4. ...it **must** be systematically planned, budgeted for and evaluated.
    5. ...each pub **must** be treated individually and on its own merits.

6. There **must** be a song about a guy named Colin somewhere...
7. These **must** be the sixth formers in the dresses.
8. Have you eaten yet? If not you **must** be very hungry.
9. Thus development communicators **must** become much more sensitive to women's problems...
10. I **must** follow my heart.
11. He **must** have been a strong contender for the Best Supporting Actor Oscar...
12. ...we **must** keep the score low to stand a chance...
13. It **must** now face the imperial impotence that Britain has found it so difficult to accept...
14. I **must** say I find it very irritating.
15. Your letter **must** state: a) Your name and class b) The length of time...

8.10 *need* and *dare*

Need and *dare* are called the 'marginal modals' because sometimes they behave as modals and sometimes as full verbs. As modals they have no third-person -s, have **inversion** for questions, are followed directly by *not* for negation, and are followed by the bare infinitive, for example:

> *Need he* worry?
> You *needn't* worry.

As full verbs they have third-person -s and past tense forms, use *do* for questions and negatives and are followed by a *to* infinitive:

> *Do we need to worry?*
> You *don't need to worry*.

The trend in modern English is to use *need* as a full verb; its modal forms are formal and some sound very strange: ?You *need* go. Dare, while relatively rare, tends still to be used as a modal, though in some cases it has the properties of both a modal and a full verb:

> I *don't dare say* what I think.

Forming the negative with *do* is characteristic of full verbs, while being followed by a bare infinitive indicates a modal.

Need and dare are also used as full, **transitive** verbs:

> I *need* you./I *dare* you.

This is very common for *need*.

Activity 8.10a

Identify in the lines below whether *need* is being used as a:

a. full verb
b. modal (and therefore formal).

Hint: look at the words following *need*.

1. If you **need** a legal eagle at midnight, there is one perched at the end of the telephone…
2. You **need** a razor blade and a white tail.
3. But I don't **need** help.
4. Indeed, for examples…one **need** look no further than Blake's own analysis…
5. …it's those inefficient producers that **need** support…
6. What we really, really **need** the public to do is get in touch with us…
7. …many [objects] do not **need** to be recorded on the database individually.
8. Flexibility and efficiency in the cost structure **need** to be maximised.
9. So, all that you **need** to think, to remember things like *don't*, is that it's *do not*…
10. [It has] everything you **need** to create great make-up looks from dawn to dusk.

Activity 8.10b

Identify in the lines below whether *dare* is being used as a:

a. full verb, or
b. modal.

Hint: look at the word following *dare*.

1. [He aimed] for speeds which other more stable pianists would never **dare** consider…
2. Don't you **dare** cry, I mumbled to myself.
3. …many people feel so ashamed of thoughts like these that they hardly **dare** express them…
4. …the range of information available…is so vast that no researcher **dare** ignore it.
5. I cry to release huge waves of feelings which can build up, especially when I cannot or **dare** not put feelings into words.
6. Walkers who would not **dare** stroll half a mile in inner cities thought nothing of walking 190 miles…
7. I hardly **dare** tell anyone.
8. I certainly wouldn't bother to test it or even **dare** to test it now.
9. …he would not have thought it possible for Senators to **dare** to do such a thing…
10. I must find another job somewhere. I'll advertise. – Don't you **dare**!

Chapter 9

Multi-word verbs

9.0 Introduction

In English a lot of common verbs are often associated with 'little words' which help to establish different meanings; in fact, they may be regarded as separate lexical items; for example, *look after*, *put off*, *turn up*:

> We invited lots of people but hardly anyone *turned up*.

These are called multi-word verbs. Usually their meaning is idiomatic in that it cannot be 'worked out' (another example) from the two parts. For example, *turn up* means 'come' or 'arrive'; there is no clue to this from either *turn* or *up*. They often have single-word synonyms: *put off* means 'postpone', for example. But although the single-word equivalents are simpler to use grammatically, they usually belong to a more formal style: *distribute* vs *hand out*, for instance.

The structure verb + 'little word' hides two grammatically distinct combinations:

1. phrasal verbs, which are a combination of verb and 'adverb particle'; for example, *put off*, *turn up*, *work out* and *hand out*:

   I've *worked out* the problem.

   The term 'phrasal verb' is sometimes applied to all multi-word verbs.

2. prepositional verbs, which are a combination of verb and preposition:

   Will you *look after* the cats while we're away?

   In this example, *after* is a preposition and in addition to combining with the verb *look* to furnish the meaning 'take care of', it also goes grammatically with the following noun phrase (*the cats*) to form a prepositional phrase.

We can see the difference between the two types if we try to move the little word:

> I've *worked* the problem *out*.
> *Will you *look* the cats *after* while we're away?

The second is not possible, because prepositions cannot normally be moved away from their noun phrase, whereas the first is possible since it is a type of adverb and is not linked to the noun phrase. This is called 'particle movement'. It is unlikely to take place if there is a long object noun phrase.

> ?I've <u>worked</u> the problem which you were talking about <u>out</u>.

But in one situation it is obligatory: when the object is a personal pronoun:

> I've <u>worked</u> it <u>out</u>. Not *I've <u>worked out</u> it.

Most of the phrasal verbs shown above are **transitive**, i.e. there is an **object**, but they can also be **intransitive**, e.g. *turn up*. In such cases particle movement is not possible of course, but they cannot be confused with prepositional verbs because there is no noun phrase to form part of a prepositional phrase.

There is a third type of multi-word verb: phrasal-prepositional verbs, where there is both an adverb particle and a preposition:

> We're <u>looking forward to</u> the end of term.

Of course, a sequence of verb and preposition may be just that, and not a prepositional verb. Compare these two examples:

> She <u>came</u> <u>across</u> the road to talk to me. (the verb *come* followed by the preposition *across*, both with their normal meanings)
> He <u>came across</u> several mistakes.   (a prepositional verb = 'find by chance')

The noun phrase following the preposition in a prepositional verb can be regarded as a kind of **object** (a **prepositional object**), and we can form a question using *who* or *what*:

> <u>What</u> did he <u>come across</u>? *Several mistakes*.

but this is unlikely with a verb + preposition combination:

> ??<u>What</u> did she <u>come across</u>? *The road*.

Passives are also possible with prepositional verbs (as of course with transitive phrasal verbs):

> How this money was <u>come by</u> we do not know.

Not all phrasal verbs are idiomatic in meaning; the verbs can have their regular meanings and some particles, especially *on* (meaning continue) and *away* (implying movement from a place), have predictable meanings; for example, *sing/play on*, *go/hurry away*.

In the rest of this chapter there is a selection of multi-word verbs that exhibit the features discussed above. In some cases, one particular combination of verb and 'little word' is focussed on; in others, one verb and a range of little words are under the spotlight. Since most of the meanings are idiomatic, you should have a good dictionary available.

9.1 *turn on*

Turn on is a rare case of a multi-word verb that can be both prepositional and phrasal, e.g.:

> I <u>turned on</u> the light./I <u>turned</u> the light <u>on</u>. (= 'switched on'; phrasal)
> The dog unexpectedly <u>turned on</u> its owner. (= 'attacked'; prepositional)

With the phrasal verb, *on* is an adverb particle; with the prepositional verb, it is a preposition and must be associated with a noun phrase ('its owner' in the above example). But in both cases the meaning is idiomatic, i.e. not predictable from the two separate words. Of course, *turn on* can also be a simple combination of two words, the single-word verb *turn* followed by the preposition *on*.

> We <u>turned</u> <u>on</u> our heels and fled.

Activity 9.1

In the lines below determine whether *turn on* is a:

a. phrasal
b. prepositional verb
c. simple combination of verb + preposition.

Hints:
- try moving *on*. If it can be moved to a position after the object then it is a phrasal verb. (*Note*: if it cannot be moved this does not mean that it is not phrasal; there may be no object, the object may be too long or it may be elsewhere in the sentence.)
- think about the meaning.

1. ...they still could not control the animals, which started to **turn on** them.
2. In their terms, however, all of these exceptions **turn on** legal concepts ...
3. ...they will automatically **turn on** lights at dusk...
4. The slopes were steep but easy to **turn on**.
5. The plots are slight and **turn on** small everyday incidents....
6. She was always eager for her **turn on** the catwalk to be over...
7. When the blood haze was on him, he could not stop killing and might **turn on** his friends once his enemies had been slaughtered.
8. It was somehow too much of an effort to lean forward and **turn on** the cold tap and besides, he wanted the heat.
9. ...the male can **turn on** the female for no apparent reason.
10. Then I **turn on** the grill to warm the place up.

9.2 *pass*

Pass can occur with a number of particles to form phrasal verbs: *on, around, over, out*; for example:

> They <u>passed</u> the documents <u>over</u> when they were ordered to.

Usually these are transitive so there is the possibility of particle movement. With some intransitive phrasal verbs there is an idiomatic meaning:

> I am afraid she has passed <u>passed</u> <u>on/away</u>. (= 'died')
> He <u>passed out</u> and fell to the floor. (= lost consciousness)

Activity 9.2

On the lines below distinguish between *pass* as a:

a. phrasal verb
b. simple verb + preposition combination.

(There are no prepositional verbs.)

Hint: try to move the little word. This will not always be possible even when it is a particle.

1. I **pass** all the correspondence I have to the County Planning Officer.
2. …[they] are positioned low-down so they **pass** beneath the cabin in the event of a severe frontal impact…
3. [These] make him believe he's in a hospital where nurses **pass** by him.
4. Radionuclides…are flushed into the sewers, from where they **pass** into watercourses…
5. **Pass** it around and when they've read it initial it and **pass** it on.
6. Please **pass** on our thanks to all the Mums, Dads and kids…
7. And we would **pass** on those benefits to the customer.
8. …you will **pass** out in a matter of seconds.
9. Currently an estimated 1,600 vessels carrying fuels and other hazardous materials **pass** through the strait annually.
10. …lapwings and shovelers nest and many waders **pass** through in spring and autumn.
11. In between we **pass** through the inevitable stages of people disappearing because they know too much.
12. Now the Linton fortune would **pass** to Isabella and her husband after Mr Edgar's death.

9.3 *look on*

Look on is another multi-word that can be both phrasal and prepositional but unlike *turn on*, the phrasal verb is intransitive so particle movement is not possible. The phrasal verb has the meaning of 'watch'; for example:

> *Everybody looked on but nobody did anything to help.*

The prepositional verb means to 'consider' or 'regard':

> *They look on us as a cash cow.*

Note the noun phrase (in this case a pronoun *us*) following the preposition. This is sometimes called a 'prepositional object'.

Activity 9.3

Decide whether *look on* on these lines is:

a. an intransitive phrasal verb
b. a prepositional verb
c. verb + preposition combinations.

Hint: ask a question beginning *Where…?* to identify verb + preposition combinations.

1. But Anselm did not **look on** himself as an agent of papal policy…
2. The hospital did not hold its breath and **look on** in admiration.
3. …organisations must **look on** insurance almost as a last resort…
4. **Look on** it as an extra bit of security for all that money you've invested…
5. She should **look on** the bright side, she kept trying to tell herself.
6. …he came to **look on** the nights…as a blessed escape.
7. One way of acquiring such ideas, of course, is to **look on** the shelves of a library…
8. But the union just **look on** us as if we are employed by them.
9. I **look on** life with a great deal of optimism…
10. He spoke in a penetrating voice that made all the other customers **look on** with interest.

9.4 *look*

Besides *look on*, a number of phrasal and prepositional verbs involve *look*. They can be phrasal, e.g. *look up*:

> Don't look up every word you don't know in a dictionary.

or prepositional, e.g. *look after*:

> Would you mind looking after the goldfish while we're away?

These multi-word verbs can be distinguished from verb + preposition combinations by forming a question with *what* or *who*:

> What are you looking up?
> What are you looking after?

whereas this is not possible with verb + preposition:

> We looked up the wall. (Where did you look? not What did you look up?)
> We looked after them walking down the road. (not Who did you look after?)

There are also some phrasal/prepositional verbs with two little words: *look up to, look down on*:

> Pupils no longer look up to their teachers.

In these cases the particle cannot be moved.

Activity 9.4

The lines below contain a sample of multi-words involving *look*. Identify them and decide whether they are phrasal, prepositional or phrasal/prepositional. If you are not familiar with the meanings check in a dictionary.

Hint: although only two words are highlighted on each line, work out if there is a third word that is important and which contributes to an idiomatic meaning.

1. Each and every employee should **look at** what they do...
2. This leaflet highlights some of the areas you need to **look at** regularly.
3. Not one of us can **look away**.
4. I could **look for** work elsewhere...
5. **Look for** toothpaste with fluoride which will help to make your teeth more resistant to attack.
6. BCRS would certainly **look forward** to any opportunity of co-operating...
7. Our friendly staff **look forward** to meeting you.
8. ...they come and **look over** the cities...
9. ...**look out** for the nifty little Sunny SR.
10. **Look out** for the 'Organically Grown' symbol.

9.5 put

Put occurs in several phrasal verbs; for example:

> They've been <u>putting off</u> this meeting for ages.
> We've <u>put forward</u> new proposals.

and as a phrasal/prepositional verb:

> Her friends <u>put</u> them <u>up for</u> membership.

Activity 9.5

On the lines below only the verb *put* has been highlighted. First of all, identify the little word it goes with – which is not always next to the verb – and then decide if it is a phrasal verb or a verb + preposition combination.

Hint: try moving the little word.

1. The company decided to **put** all its litigation work, worth over a million pounds a year, out to tender.
2. ...a quick way to re-test the system is to **put** all that test data in again...
3. Ten years ago, surveys showed people were willing to **put** in a half-hour in the kitchen.
4. [They] should never have been **put** into operation.
5. I've **put** it in my diary.
6. I've just **put** my house on the market in York...
7. And I **put** that down to the biggest contribution.
8. ...the agent said she thought I'd **put** the phone down.
9. ...**put** the stuff back in the box...
10. **Put** the resolution to the meeting.
11. I've **put** the kettle on.
12. ...it **put** up venture capital for an 11% stake early last year.

9.6 set

Set occurs in a number of phrasal verbs; for example:

> *Winter has already <u>set in</u>.* (intransitive)
> *The new laws <u>set down</u> standards of public behaviour.* (transitive)

It is also focussed on in 7.4 with regard to its verb patterns.

Activity 9.6

On the lines below all of the verb + little word combinations, except one, are phrasal verbs. Which one is the exception?

Hint: try moving the little word (though this will not identify all the phrasal verbs).

1. ...the English court has **set aside** convictions resting upon identification...
2. ...we've **set aside** a room...
3. General availability of the completed...release is **set for** mid-1993.
4. We got some torches together and **set off** for the graveyard.
5. ...paragraphs 3 to 5 **set out** the functions of the adjudicator.
6. She **set out** to play the world circuit completely on her own...
7. The European Commission has **set up** definitive measures to stop imports...
8. We must **set up** processes of measurement...

9.7 come

Come is used in many phrasal, prepositional and phrasal/prepositional verbs:

> *<u>Come in</u> and sit down.* (phrasal)
> *How did you <u>come by</u> that?* (prepositional)
> *They didn't <u>come up to</u> much.* (phrasal/prepositional)

or it may be a verb + preposition combination:

> *<u>Come in</u> the house and get warm.*

Activity 9.7

Decide whether *come* on the following lines is phrasal, prepositional, phrasal/prepositional or a verb + preposition combination. In particular, work out whether the prepositions are part of a prepositional verb (where they contribute to an idiomatic meaning) or are simply being used normally after a single-word or phrasal verb. Only the verb and following word are highlighted below; there may be another word of interest.

Hint: trying to ask a question about the following noun phrase may help to distinguish prepositional verbs from verb + preposition combinations; if only *what* is possible then it is a prepositional verb.

1. ...that increase in production has **come about** through the use of technology...
2. This has **come about** partly because our main brand...is able to complement the lager type beers...
3. ...you might **come across** that in your reading.
4. Have you **come across** this criticism as you go round the area?
5. If you have any side effects from the new ones, then you should **come back** straight away.
6. I knew you would **come back** into the house, so please take some food.
7. For example, we now...encourage them to actually **come forward** with their complaints...
8. ...members would **come from** a variety of backgrounds.
9. I see an awful lot of women who obviously **come in** for some slight improvement...
10. Eels **come into** it somehow, but not in a way that can be described in a family newspaper.
11. If you'd like to **come into** the office, perhaps I could help you to search.
12. What they do find difficult is filling their day once they have actually **come off** drugs...
13. Different parts of the lighting system can **come on** at different times.
14. **Come on**, nearly everybody ought to be able to work this one out now.
15. Would you **come over** to that bench over there?
16. ...recent research has **come to** the same conclusions as Golding...
17. Both sides know that eventually it will **come to** a fight.
18. Now that's a question that we can all **come up** with at times...
19. ...they used to...**come up** here in the summer and sell them.
20. It will **come with** what may well seem a comprehensive range of facilities.

9.8 get over

Get over can be both a phrasal and prepositional verb. As a prepositional verb it means 'recover from'/'deal with':

> *Get over it and stop complaining.*

As a phrasal verb it means 'finish' or 'convey':

> *Come on then, let's get the deal over and done with.*

This example exhibits an unusual feature of some transitive phrasal verbs: that the particle always comes after the object (so not *let's get over the deal...*).

Activity 9.8

On these lines distinguish between the use of *get over* as a:

a. phrasal verb
b. prepositional verb
c. verb + preposition combination.

Hint: try asking questions with *what*.

1. Now if you can **get over** the main point of that story in two words, I'm sure you can **get over** the main point of any of those stories in thirty seconds.
2. ...as soon as Leeds **get over** 50 points (whenever that is) there is a celebration.
3. A support group has been set up to help animal lovers **get over** the death of a pet.
4. ...they couldn't **get over** the fact that I didn't like ice in whisky...
5. If you can't **get over** yourself, can you send Maradona?
6. ...try as she might Theresa simply could not **get over** losing him.
7. [He was] a little black and white Border collie pup, so small he could only just manage to **get over** the doorstep.
8. Nobody likes to be inspected and we've had to **get over** that initial hurdle.

9.9 *go*

Go is most frequently used as an intransitive single-word verb, indicating motion:

We can go any time you want.

But it is also common as an intransitive phrasal verb:

Let's go away for the weekend

and as a prepositional verb:

Let's go over the details later.

Note that *over* is a preposition here, attached to the following noun phrase.

Activity 9.9

Distinguish the following uses of *go* on the lines below:

  a. intransitive single-word verb
  b. intransitive phrasal verb
  c. prepositional verb.

Hint: check the word that follows *go*; it may not be a particle or preposition.

1. I am putting together an album of our preservation activities as we **go** along...
2. I'd like to **go** back to some of the comments that were made earlier...
3. ...most would **go** further and admit that it is absurd...
4. ...the Air Raid siren used to **go** off at night...
5. I **go** out on Monday and get everything else for the week like washing powder...
6. And did you say your brothers didn't **go** there though, they went to a different school?
7. The corporation hopes miners will...not **go** through the lengthy procedure.
8. One can **go** to conferences where one is being talked at most of the time.

Chapter 10

Question words, relative words and subordinators

10.0 Introduction

We now come to a small group of words that are very important in English grammar.

They are important because they serve three very different functions. These words are *which, who, whom, whose, what, when, where, why* and *how*. They are sometimes called 'wh-words' because they all start with those two letters (with *how* as an honorary member).

As question words – sometimes called 'interrogatives' – they introduce one type of interrogative sentence:

> *Who are you seeing tonight?*

These are called *wh-* questions (as opposed to *yes/no* questions and other types).

As relative words – sometimes called 'relativisers' – they introduce **relative clauses**, which function as the **postmodification** of noun phrases:

> *Is that the girl who you are seeing tonight?*

Two words in this group, *what* and *how*, do not function as relative words. As subordinators they introduce **nominal** or **adverbial subordinate clauses**. In nominal subordinate clauses the clause acts as something like a noun phrase, answering the questions *what...?* or *who...?*:

> *I know who you are seeing tonight.* (cf. *What do you know?*)

In this example the subordinate clause functions as the **object** of *know* in the main clause. It may also (but less commonly) function as the **subject** of the main clause:

> *Who you are seeing tonight does not interest me.*

or the **predicative**:

> *So that is who you are seeing tonight.*

Adverbial subordinate clauses function as **adverbials** in the main clause:

> *I'll tell you my secret when the time is right.*
> *She was sitting where she shouldn't have been.*

In this they are similar to subordinating conjunctions in general; for example, *because*:

> *I'll tell you because you deserve to know.*

Table 10.1 wh-words functions and word classes

	Question word	Relative word	Subordinator
which	✓ (pn, det)	✓ (pn, det?)	✓ (pn, det)
who	✓ (pn)	✓ (pn)	✓ (pn)
whom	✓ (pn)	✓ (pn)	✓ (pn)
whose	✓ (pn, det)	✓ (det)	✓ (pn, det)
what	✓ (pn, det)		✓ (pn, det)
when	✓ (adverb)	✓ (adverb)	✓ (adverb)
where	✓ (adverb)	✓ (adverb)	✓ (adverb)
why	✓ (adverb)	✓ (adverb)	✓ (adverb)
how	✓ (adverb)		✓ (adverb)

(pn = pronoun, det = determiner)

These three functions cut across the traditional word class distinctions in terms of word class pronoun, determiner and adverb. Table 10.1 shows the different functions and word classes of these words.

One other word which could have been included here: *that*, since it is used as both relative word and subordinator. However, it is also used as a determiner and pronoun and so is included in Chapter 12.

10.1 *which*

Which is used in all three ways. As a question word it asks about a **definite** noun phrase. It can act either as a pronoun:

> *Which did you choose?*

or as a determiner:

> *Which shoes did you choose?*

As a relative word it is almost always a pronoun:

> *It was the last song which made me cry.*

Its use as a determiner is archaic, except in expressions:

> *He may be a crook, in which case you should hang on to your money.*

Mention should also be made of its role as a sentential relative, where it is referring back not to the preceding noun phrase (the 'antecedent') but to the whole clause:

> *Then he slipped and fell, which made everyone laugh.*

As a subordinator it can be a pronoun:

> *Do you know which is ours?*

or a determiner:

> *Do you know which umbrella is ours?*

In these examples the nominal subordinate clause functions as the object of the main verb, *know*. *Which* can also introduce a subject:

> <u>Which school we choose</u> will affect their future.

Activity 10.1

On the following lines work out whether *which* is a:

a. question word
b. relative word
c. subordinator.

Also distinguish its determiner and pronoun uses.

Hint: try replacing *which* with *that*.

1. AIDS is a sensitive area **which** many schools are unsure how to tackle.
2. …they are concerned with the judge's actions and decisions **which** led up to his discharge of the jury.
3. **Which** union is it that you're in?
4. …the small investor at last has a choice of funds **which** follow share indices.
5. Accordingly, he has drawn up a document outlining his position on negotiations **which** he means to make public…
6. Spaceprints is making you an offer **which** is too good to miss.
7. There's a very interesting table **which** is now produced by the D of E…
8. We have also developed meat and egg trays **which** are CFC-free…
9. It is not a long-term strategy upon **which** Europe can depend.
10. A guide to the contents of this Workbook, **which** are also subject to change…, is to be found in Appendix A.
11. But she did confirm that they had been deposited in the Kazachi Aquarium, **which** is surrounded by military bases…
12. I like the texture of that other one. – **Which** one?
13. Scottish Opera's current Marriage of Figaro, **which** opened at the Theatre Royal in Glasgow on Thursday, is unlikely to cause offence or rouse strong passions.
14. …then I read this amazing article **which** said 'no', it's completely the other way around…
15. This notice will tell us **which** floor it's on.

10.2 who

Who is used in all three ways to refer to people. As a question word, it functions as a pronoun representing the subject:

> <u>Who</u> did this?

or the predicative:

> <u>Who</u> is that? (*That's Darren.*)

or the object:

> _Who_ did you see?

As a relative word, it can act as the subject or object of the relative clause that it introduces:

> We're looking for someone _who loves children_. (subject)
> We're looking for someone _who we can trust_. (object)

It is not used as a relative determiner.

As a subordinator it can introduce an object nominal clause:

> I know _who did this_.

or a subject nominal clause:

> _Who gets the prize_ hasn't yet been decided.

In all three uses _who_ cannot occur after prepositions: *_At who_ did you look? (But _Who_ did you look _at_?)

Activity 10.2

On these lines distinguish between the use of _who_ as a:

a. question word
b. relative word
c. subordinator.

Hint: try replacing _who_ (as a relative pronoun) with _that_.

1. ... and as usual our thanks to all **who** worked so hard to make it successful.
2. And **who** were they?
3. ...and **who** would replace them in their respective jobs if they go?
4. There is a rapidly growing number in Britain **who** regard dolphins in captivity as similar to humans in slavery.
5. Defendants **who** are found guilty of any drug-selling offence may be stripped of all their assets...
6. What a wonderful vision the lady **who** lives at the top of our road shared with us all.
7. They do not discuss **who** is saying what in de Man's work.
8. ...in every relationship there is one **who** loves and one who is loved...
9. ...these patients were pretty much equally split between patients **who** had obstruction and patients who did not...
10. This is for those people **who** think they aren't properly dressed...
11. We buy up the files...and see **who** the lucky person is.
12. Policies such as these penalise those **who** drink sensibly...
13. But some of the Tories **who** successfully rebelled last year, showed their disappointment.
14. He is not the sort of person **who** sits on the sidelines giving instructions.
15. **Who** does Marion live with?

10.3 *whom*

The first thing that needs to be said about *whom* is that it is infrequent and very formal, and in most cases it can be – and is – avoided. Historically it functioned fully as the **objective** form of *who*, and still does in very formal circumstances, but usually it is replaced by *who*.

In all cases it refers to people. It is used as a question word, denoting the object of the sentence:

Whom are you discussing? (Also Who...?)

as a relative word, denoting the object of the relative clause:

That is the woman whom you are discussing. (Also ...who..., etc.)

or as a subordinator, introducing a nominal subordinate clause in which it represents the object:

I know whom you are discussing. (Also ...who...)

There is one condition under which *whom* has to be used: when it follows a **preposition**, for example:

That is the woman about whom you are talking. (relative word)
I know about whom you are talking. (subordinator)

(Not *...*about who* you are talking...*, but *...who you are talking about* is possible in both cases.)

Activity 10.3

a. Say whether *whom* could be replaced by *who* on these lines.
b. Identify whether *whom* is a question word, a relative word, or a subordinator.

Hint: look at the word that precedes *whom* (ignoring the preposition if there is one).

1. He couldn't see someone about **whom** he knew nothing.
2. ...of the 13 who stated a preference at first interview for home care and **whom** we were able to interview again..., six stated an unequivocal preference for home care...
3. Sir John Markham was married three times; first to Anne, daughter of Sir George Neville, by **whom** he had three sons...
4. John had always a group of dancers within the company **whom** he particularly liked to work with...
5. [The judge said he] was...a dangerous young man for **whom** a determinate sentence was not appropriate...
6. West Ham will be at home to Derby, for **whom** their former striker Paul Goddard is such an important figure.
7. Henry gave Richard the task of quelling the very Aquitainian rebels from **whom** he had so recently looked for support.
8. ...I therefore wrote to Eliot, from **whom** I had not heard further...

9. ...the required hostage should be none other than Seton's own son, a young man **whom** he had brought with him...
10. His second wife Maria, **whom** he married in 1849, was the daughter of William Hawkins of the Madras Civil Service.
11. ...good news was on the way for the mostly small depositors, many of **whom** lost their life savings...
12. I'm going to waste my time visiting two dealers, both of **whom** will try to sell me items I don't want...
13. Please let us never condemn...the parents to **whom** the strength is not given.
14. Here are the addresses of prisoners to **whom** they can be sent...
15. ...he had a constant stream of visitors with **whom** he discussed his ideas...

10.4 *whose*

Whose it used in all three ways to refer to people who are involved in possession or some other relationship. As a question word it can be a determiner:

Whose gloves are those?

or a pronoun:

Whose are those?

It is equivalent to a **possessive pronoun/determiner** or a **genitive**. Thus, an answer to the above two examples could be:

They are mine.
They are my gloves.
They are Darren's gloves.

As a relative word it is only used as a determiner:

Is that the lecturer whose class you failed?

The relative clause (*whose class I failed*) postmodifies the noun *lecturer*.
   As a subordinator it typically introduces object nominal clauses:

Do we know whose car it is?

or less frequently subject nominal clauses:

Whose idea it was doesn't matter now.

Activity 10.4

On these lines work out whether *whose* is a:

a. question word
b. relative word
c. subordinator.

Hint: check what precedes *whose*.

1. Using this process we can personalise the letter to every adviser **whose** details have been recorded on our agency records.
2. The figure **whose** character achieved clearest focus was that of Fulk the Good…
3. Farming is a major industry **whose** importance to maintaining the health of rural life…is all too easily forgotten.
4. …the client feels that he is in the hands of an expert, into **whose** capable hands all matters concerned with the funeral can be safely delivered.
5. …it consists mainly of mothers **whose** husbands, sons and daughters have disappeared…
6. [It was] a lasting and practical memorial to the much-loved British musician **whose** name it bears.
7. Whose job is it to look after people **whose** bodies are incapacitated, for one reason or another?
8. Gavin could check the list of names and see **whose** mail IT is reading?
9. Nigel Parriss, **whose** brainchild it all has been, was amazed by the amount of interest…
10. The bid is being resisted by Pearl Group, **whose** chairman…has described the offer as derisory…
11. Then Mr Utterson at last turned and looked at his companion, **whose** face was as pale as his own.
12. It claims that several hundred, **whose** names are unknown, are believed to be in prison.
13. Asterix, **whose** village was the last in Gaul to resist the invading Romans, was conceived in the Fifties…
14. The murdered tourist left a widow, **whose** permission was not asked before the work was written.
15. …special thanks to the Princess Royal, without **whose** leadership it would not have been possible at all.

10.5 *what*

What is used as a question word and a subordinator. As a question word it asks about an **indefinite** noun phrase. It can either be a pronoun:

> *What have you been up to?*

or a determiner:

> *What mischief have you been up to?*

As a subordinator it introduces a nominal subordinate clause:

> *I don't know what you were expecting.*

In this example, the subordinate clause functions as the object of *know* in the main clause, and *what* itself functions as the object of *expect* in the subordinate clause (*expect something*).
  The clause can also be a subject:

> *What we were expecting was a better performance.*

or a predicative:

> *This is what we were expecting.*

What does not function as a relative word. However, it does occur in **exclamations**:

> *What a nice day it is!*

Activity 10.5

On the lines below, distinguish the use of *what* as a:

a. question word
b. subordinator.

Regarding the latter, say what kind of nominal clause it is introducing:

c. a subject
d. a predicative
e. an object.

Hint: try replacing *what* with *the thing that*.

1. 'But **what** can we do?' said Jason.
2. We'll get it cut off and put in the bin, that's **what** they'll do with it.
3. …that's exactly **what** you're doing.
4. Do you want to know **what's** happening to our countryside…?
5. …people that haven't experienced it don't know **what** they're talking about.
6. So **what** kind of…research goes into choosing where to actually site one?
7. **What** we're actually doing…is we're actually widening the franchise…
8. **What** am I going to say now? Erm, **what** was your job exactly?
9. Well now, **what** can I do for you today?
10. …**what** I'm trying to say is that they have a vital role…
11. We do not know yet **what** causes a cell to become cancerous…
12. **What** happened in the 1980s was a temporary aberration…

10.6 *when*

When is used in all three ways:

1. As a question word it functions as an adverbial of time:

   When did it happen? (last night)

2. As a relative word it introduces a relative subordinate clause:

   This is the day <u>when all our work will be rewarded</u>.

3. As a subordinator it can introduce both nominal and adverbial subordinate clauses:

   I don't know <u>when I'll see you again</u>. (nominal, object)
   Give me your answer <u>when you've thought about it</u>. (adverbial)

Activity 10.6

On these lines distinguish the following uses of *when*:

a. question word
b. relative word
c. subordinator.

Hint: try replacing the clause introduced by *when* with *then* (you may need to turn the sentence round).

1. **When** it comes to enjoying yourself in Ontario, there's just one problem.
2. I had one night of that, and **when** he came round in the morning, I told him.
3. 'And **when** we want to leave, you'll give it back, won't you?' she asked.
4. [He left] the college on a sounder footing…than it had been **when** he took office.
5. You may see traces of blood **when** you brush your teeth.
6. I had donkeys **when** I was in Forres, 23 years ago…
7. …the eldest child was four years old **when** he came to this country…
8. …hopefully he will carry it on **when** the time comes.
9. **When** we are in need we can forget all about other people.
10. I think **when** it comes to bearing selection issues we ought to be clear which direction we're going in…
11. I'm grateful that I was born **when** I was…
12. **When** we are facing away from the sun what happens?
13. And it's always a worry **when** you don't know what's going on.
14. He had this meeting on Wake Island…**when** they wouldn't get out of the planes…
15. I would like to go back to the days of my youth **when** at Hogmanay there was usually frost and ice…

10.7 *where*

Where is used in all three ways.

1. As a question word it functions as an adverb of place (i.e. a **central adverb**):

   Where did you put it? (= 'in what place?')

2. As a relative word it introduces a clause which postmodifies a noun indicating location:

   There are places where you can still see the bullet holes.

3. As a subordinator it can introduce nominal subordinate clauses, either as the object:

   Let me know where you're staying.

   or subject:

   Where you park doesn't matter.

   or predicative:

   This is where I catch the bus.

It can also introduce adverbial clauses:

You can sit where you like.

Activity 10.7

Distinguish on these lines between the use of *where* as a:

a. question word
b. relative word
c. subordinator (and in this case between the different types of nominal clause).

Hint: try replacing *where* with *there*.

1. And **where** do I go then...?
2. ...he says that there may be cases **where** there aren't enough people of independent means...
3. [They] take account of the laws...in the countries **where** the employees live and work.
4. Okay, so **where** shall we start?
5. So her hands were up and they were off before I knew **where** they were.
6. ...at least they might know **where** to draw the line.
7. ...the future for the school cannot be as bright as it is for one **where** they are working as a team.
8. ...foolishly I moved to a place **where** I had a full view of the stage.
9. **Where** can you gain the information...if you can't see the roundabout?
10. That's **where** I live.
11. I would go there, simply because of the situation **where** the TV never is switched off.
12. 'So **where** are we now?' asked Zanya.
13. I've got a photograph somewhere **where** we had this trestle table on the platform...
14. One of the biggest operations is at Fettes...., **where** the restaurant is open throughout the day...
15. **Where** will I go for the scan?

10.8 *why*

As a question word *why* functions as an adverbial:

Why did he do it? ('For what reason...')

As a subordinator it introduces nominal subordinate clauses:

I don't know why he did it. (object)
Why he did it is irrelevant. (subject)
This is why no one trusts them. (predicative)

As a relative word its status is marginal; it may follow *reason*:

That is the reason why she left.

Activity 10.8

Distinguish on these lines the use of *why* as a:

a. question word
b. relative word
c. subordinator. For the subordinators, distinguish the different types of subordinate clause that they introduce.

Hint: look at the position of *why*.

1. …why does iron rust, for example?
2. That is why we have got to aim to have programmes that cherish diversity and originality.
3. I don't know why I should think you know what women want…
4. …why is it people put so much pressure on you to get married?
5. You didn't know what was happening or why.
6. And I think that's probably why people find it frustrating.
7. Now the other reason why…you won't perhaps drive naturally is because of this little bit of tension…
8. That's why he hates the garden so much…
9. I understood why people were frightened, why they shouted and threw stones.
10. …that was why they were so determined to win.
11. Inspector, why didn't your men shoot?
12. …why did they make soles of it?
13. …it makes me wonder why we've got money on deposit in a bank.
14. Why is an elephant big and grey and wrinkly? Because if it was small and white and smooth it would be an aspirin!
15. And the passage we are to look at today made me ask several 'Why?' questions.

10.9 *how*

How is used in several ways. As a question word it functions as a **central adverb** of manner:

> *How did you manage that?* ('In what way…?')

As a subordinator it introduces nominal subordinate clauses:

> *I'll tell you how I did it later.* (object nominal)
> *How I did it is a secret.* (subject nominal)

It is also used as a degree adverb, modifying adjectives and adverbs, both as a question word and subordinator:

> *How big is it?* (question word)
> *I don't know how big it is.* (subordinator)

It often occurs in phrasal *wh-* words: *how often, how long, how much/many*:

> *How often do you eat here?*

and in *how about* to make a suggestion:

> *How about a film tonight?*

This should be treated as one item.

It does not function as a relative word. However, it does occur in **exclamations**:

> *How wonderful you look!*

Activity 10.9

On these lines for *how* work out first of all whether it is a:

a. question word
b. subordinator
c. part of an exclamation.

Then identify whether it is a:

d. central adverb or
e. degree adverb.

Note: this distinction cuts across the previous one.

Hint: try replacing *how* with *the way in which*.

1. There are various calculations about **how** much land is potentially redundant…
2. And two families discover **how** the divide between the two is narrowing.
3. **How** many people did they employ there?
4. **How** much do the louvres cost as a proportion…?
5. **How** about the works dances? What were they like?
6. **How** can you draw a picture representing land?
7. **How** do you treat somebody who's had carbon monoxide poisoning?
8. …**how** on earth can we actually do anything…?
9. **How** stupid I was!
10. Now we said that the earth rotates once in **how** many hours?
11. [That] is **how** the business is today.
12. …you already know **how** to use them.
13. I'll phone you once a week and you can tell me **how** you're getting on.
14. I've got very dim memories of **how** it actually started…
15. …keep an eye on **how** well it's working.
16. **How** can it benefit crop production?
17. Mr Healey was remarking **how** very few people bothered to vote there at all…
18. …it just shows **how** interested some of us are…
19. …**how** many people do they have with your particular background…?
20. And you wonder **how** it would ever be any good at anything.

Chapter 11

Multi-functional words (1)

11.0 Introduction

This chapter deals with words that do not fit easily into the previous word-class-based chapters since they belong to several word classes. This multi-functionality is a feature of many English words, especially the more common ones. We have already seen a number of words that belong to more than one word class, in particular in Chapter 3, where several of the determiners and pronouns there could also be used as adverbs. For some grammarians this multiple word-class membership is an argument against the whole concept of word class as a way of describing English grammar; for others the difference in word class is a useful tool for describing the varying behaviour of many words.

The words in this chapter are something of a mixed bag; there is little that holds them together, apart from the fact that they all belong to at least one of the major content word classes: noun, adjective or verb (as well as to function word classes), and it is such meanings that typically come to mind (e.g. *round* as an adjective meaning 'circular'), even though it is the functional uses that are usually more common. Beyond that, there are no generalisations that can be made about them. In some cases the differences between the various uses of one form are so great that they can be regarded as different words, even though the spelling and pronunciation are identical, i.e. as cases of homonymy.

Chapter 12 deals with similar multiple word-class words that have no content word-class membership.

11.1 *round*

Round is used in several different ways, but most have the idea of circles or circularity. The stereotype is that *round* is an adjective (*The ball is round*), but this use in fact is very rare, as the lines below demonstrate.

The main uses of *round* are as an adverb particle in phrasal verbs (see Chapter 9):

>   I'll go <u>round</u> and see her later.

and as a preposition, part of a prepositional phrase answering the question *where*:

>   A number of spectators were standing <u>round the field</u>.

The distinction between the preposition and adverb particle uses is very slim. It is only the presence or absence of the following noun phrase that distinguishes their grammar; the meaning is basically the same.

He walked round (the room).

In these two uses *round* can be replaced by *around*.
  Round is also used:

- as an adverb postmodifying noun phrases:

Have a good look round.

- as a verb, especially as a part of a phrasal verb:

Let's round the bill up.

- as a noun, meaning 'one stage in a series of events':

He lost in the first round.

- as an adjective:

Cricket pitches can be round or oval.

Apart from the first of these uses, *around* cannot replace *round*.

Activity 11.1

Identify whether *round* on the following lines is:

a. a preposition
b. an adverb particle
c. an adverb postmodifying a noun
d. a verb
e. a noun.

Hint: try replacing *round* with *around*.

1. They're in orbit. Orbit means you go **round** and **round**…
2. I turned **round** and saw Mr Ross.
3. There are other reports of foxes collecting **round** farmhouses to scavenge.
4. He'd got a pole, with a bear dancing **round** it.
5. The Local Residents' Group was sending **round** its poison print-outs…
6. Few…expect that the development effort will survive the next **round** of cuts.
7. Traditionally mature, full-bodied red wines…have been drunk with cheese to **round** off a meal.
8. …it will be exactly as it is now having gone all the way **round**…
9. I hung his clothes **round** the boiler fire.
10. You hear him **round** the corner…
11. He finished his fish, got up, put his arm **round** Tildy…
12. I have come **round** to thinking that small country schools should be kept open…
13. You didn't get time to go **round** to everybody…
14. …he went hunting **round** Woodstock quite often…
15. You, you must be **round** your ideal weight really.

11.2 *back*

Back is often thought of as referring to a part of the body, but in fact it is most commonly used as an adverb particle with phrasal verbs:

> *We fly <u>back</u> at the end of the month.*

See Chapter 9 on phrasal verbs for more information.
It can also be:

- an adverb:

> *We'll be <u>back</u> in a moment.*

Note that it is not an adjective here (it cannot be placed in front of a noun).

- a noun:

> *The <u>back</u> of the chair needs repairing.*

- an adjective:

> *I was ushered into the <u>back</u> room.*

- a verb:

> *If I stand for election, will you <u>back</u> me?*

Activity 11.2

Decide whether *back* on these lines is:

- a. an adverb particle
- b. an adverb
- c. a noun
- d. an adjective
- e. a verb.

Hint: work out which word *back* goes with.

1. I'm glad we went **back** and shared the news...
2. They're not square at the **back**!
3. ...we went out full but now she comes **back** empty.
4. Fly through the air and you're **back** in the square!
5. She'd put too much weight on it, and she's **back** in hospital...
6. I want you **back** in four weeks.
7. You know the little box that goes into the **back** of the telly.
8. Liverpool dockers recently turned **back** parts of a 1,500-tonne consignment...
9. But they might find it difficult to take a **back** seat...
10. ...I wonder if I could go **back** to that point that...you raised this morning...
11. ...so I'll probably give it **back** to you in a couple of minutes.
12. Straight away, he rushed **back** to the village with his extraordinary tale.

13. The coach was nice and comfy, with a toilet at the **back**…
14. I need to **back** up for a moment perhaps.
15. The second wild cat ran **back** up into the mountains.

11.3 *down*

The main use of *down* is as an adverb particle with phrasal verbs:

Sit <u>down</u> for a moment.

The verb may be intransitive, as above, or transitive with an object, in which case *down* may be moved:

They're cutting <u>down</u> the trees/the trees <u>down</u>.

See Chapter 9 for more information on this.
   It is also used as:

- an 'ordinary' adverb of place:

We're <u>down</u> in London next weekend.

- a preposition preceding a noun phrase:

She walked <u>down</u> the street without looking back.

- occasionally as an adjective, verb or noun:

I'm feeling <u>down</u> at the moment. (adjective)
I bet you can't <u>down</u> that in one go. (verb)

Activity 11.3

Identify whether *down* on these lines is:

a. an adverb particle
b. an adverb
c. a preposition
d. a verb.

Hint: try moving *down*. In this way phrasal verbs where there is an object (but not those where there is no object) will be distinguished from prepositions.

1. …they are responsible for laying **down** a code of conduct for their members…
2. I got a little excited and told him to quietly shut the engine **down**…
3. Louise, just put your pen **down** and join with this please.
4. …when he's **down** at his granny's, my mummy and my daddy are actually talking…
5. Miranda looked **down** at the stones below.
6. But the orders come **down** from above and we jump to it.
7. She'll swallow that **down** nice and gently and it'll coat her tummy…
8. Presumably they pick up the pint of milk and **down** the sherry and beer as well…

9. ...a number of Yorkshire law firms...are sending a chill **down** the back of the London legal establishment.
10. I think you've got a really nasty infection **down** there.
11. He will implement procedures laid **down** to comply with the Company's duty of care...
12. For every tree which is chopped **down**, up to 6 more are planted in its place.

11.4 *right*

Right belongs to a number of content word classes. It is most commonly used as an adjective either meaning 'correct'/'appropriate'; for example:

> That's the *right* spirit!

or the opposite of *left*.

In spoken English it is frequently used as a 'discourse marker', to show that an old topic is over and a new stage of conversation is being started:

> *Right*, are there any questions?

It can also be:

- an adverb meaning 'directly' or 'fully':

> The sun was shining *right* into my eyes.

- a noun:

> People should have a *right* to clean water.

- a verb:

> It's not easy to *right* every wrong.

Activity 11.4

Decide on these lines whether *right* is:

a. an adjective
b. an adverb
c. a discourse marker
d. a noun.

Hint: try replacing *right* with *correct* or *directly*.

1. ...a lot of these drugs are not without potential side effects. – That's **right**.
2. ...you can be sure to find something that's just **right** for you...
3. Is it still up this arm mostly? The **right** one?
4. It goes **right** into there.
5. **Right**, let's have a wee look here and see if we can make it sore.
6. So, four weeks? – **Right**, see you in four weeks.

7. I want to get the **right** sort of thing for you.
8. But I reckon they have got it just **right** with the Mondeo.
9. Doing all the **right** things is not enough!
10. Work at Whessoe Road will go on **right** through the summer.
11. Everyone has the **right** to freedom of opinion and expression…
12. …she doesn't say a lot, but she says the **right** things.

11.5 *well*

Well is usually thought of as the irregular adverb related to *good*; for example:

   Beat the eggs <u>well</u>.

In this it is often preceded by intensifiers:

   That didn't go <u>too</u> <u>well</u>.

But it is also common as a discourse marker, to indicate a speaker has been thinking about what they are going to say next:

   <u>*Well*</u>, *I wouldn't believe everything she says.*

It is also used:

* as an adjective, meaning 'in good health':

   I haven't been feeling <u>well</u> lately.

* in expressions: *as well as, well done*.
* as a noun, which may be regarded as a different word:

   The ground is too hard to dig a <u>well</u>.

Activity 11.5

Identify whether *well* on these lines is:

   a. a discourse marker
   b. an adverb
   c. an adjective
   d. an expression.

Hint: work out which word *well* goes with, if any.

1. I have found it better to do a small area really **well** and then concentrate on another…
2. [It] might even damage them as **well** as the rest of the environment.
3. **Well** how can I describe it to you?
4. Indeed several graduates have done exceptionally **well** in Livewire…
5. …one or two of you seem to think you didn't do too **well** in April…
6. Now he's otherwise fit and **well**, isn't he?
7. **Well** it wouldn't make any difference.
8. **Well** they'll be asking the rest of us to take a cut in salary soon.

9. **Well**, what can I do for you today, Agnes?
10. ...it burned for me quite **well** when dry.
11. And I'm sure it'd be **well** worth getting this down...

11.6 *past*

Past belongs to three word classes. It can be:

- a noun:

  The <u>past</u> is another country.

- an adjective:

  <u>Past</u> experience tells me it won't succeed.

- a preposition, followed by a noun phrase to make a prepositional phrase:

  He looked straight <u>past</u> me.

  especially with times of the day, meaning 'after':

  half <u>past</u> nine.

Activity 11.6

Decide whether *past* on these lines is

a. an adjective
b. a preposition
c. a noun.

Hint: work out the relationship between *past* and the noun phrase. Is it the head, a premodifier or outside the noun phrase?

1. ...we have been operating 365 days a year, for the **past** 24 years.
2. [It is] presumably reprised as a nod to her unhappy **past** acquaintance with the bottle.
3. [This] holds the key to our **past**, and our future.
4. Over these **past** couple of weeks we've been looking at some of the questions...
5. Ask banks, building societies, former landlords, present and **past** employers.
6. ...he said not all religious orders have been so generous in the **past**.
7. Yes, well we had to dig from half **past** nine in the morning...
8. In the **past**, he says, the company was at a disadvantage...
9. In February, it swept **past** Jupiter with British instruments on board...
10. [...it] has been widely leaked over the **past** month.
11. ...the crews will be...coming over and then **past** my window again.
12. ...every time someone drove **past** the picket line, there was a bit of bad publicity...
13. That's all right, he said, and walked along the road, **past** the prison.
14. It was half **past** two in the morning.
15. When we arrived at my friend's house, a young man hurried **past** us...

11.7 *light*

Light is an interesting word. It belongs to the three major content word classes: noun, verb and adjective. But within each class there are yet more major differences.

As a noun, it is both count and noncount with different meanings (see Chapter 1), for example:

> *This process turns light into heat.* (noncount = the physical phenomenon)
> *A light was still shining in his room.* (count, something which supplies light)

As an adjective it has a number of different meanings; for example, as the opposite of 'heavy', 'dark' and 'serious':

> *There's only light traffic at this time of the day.* (= not heavy)

As a verb, it can be both transitive and intransitive (and phrasal):

> *You prepare the food while I light the barbecue.*
> *His face will light up when I tell him the news.*

Activity 11.7

Decide whether *light* on these lines is:

a. a noncount noun
b. a count noun
c. an adjective (and which meaning it has)
d. a verb.

Hint: work out the relationship between *light* and neighbouring words.

1. ...it was full of golden **light** and the sun was sitting in it...
2. The rain will turn **light** and patchy...
3. You must keep to **light**, plain colours.
4. For a **light** car, the AX rides surprisingly well...
5. ...please turn the **light** off after them.
6. In this article I intend to shed some **light** on the behaviour of a specific linguistic phenomenon...
7. Although many of the calls are routine, we do have moments of **light** relief.
8. ...quite a bit of that heat is coming off as **light**.
9. ...there was a clock in the **light** room which struck every five minutes...
10. We **light** this candle on the third Sunday of Advent.
11. ...your hair dryer doesn't **light** up when you put electricity through it, does it?
12. A little grey **light** was coming in through the window.

11.8 *like*

Like has two main uses. In this case the two are so dissimilar that they may be considered different words: a case of homonymy.

It is most common as a preposition meaning 'for example':

> I've been to lots of places, _like_ Thailand, Vietnam, China...

or 'similar to'; for instance:

> Children grow to be _like_ their parents.

In this meaning it can also be a conjunction:

> Do we still think _like_ we used to?

As a conjunction is also common after verbs of perception to express a deduction:

> It _looks like_ the game is over.

In recent years a new use of this version of _like_ has become popular among young people, the so-called 'quotative _like_'. It is used to introduce some reported words or thought:

> So he walks away and I'm _like_ 'Hey, dude, where's my money?'

This can be understood as 'I'm thinking/saying something like...'. Some people object to this use but it is very common.

The other major use of _like_ is as a transitive verb:

> Everybody _likes_ a big spender – until his money runs out.

Rather than having a noun phrase as an object, it can be followed by an infinitive, or noun phrase + infinitive:

> I'd _like to agree_ with you.
> We'd _like our son to study_ music.

Activity 11.8

Identify whether _like_ on the following lines is:

a. a preposition
b. a conjunction
c. quotative
d. a verb.

Hint: try replacing like with _similar to_.

1. ...they say it has become **like** a jungle.
2. ...nothing revives the hardworking executive **like** a glass of Scotch...
3. It's gone **like** a dream...
4. And do you get any perks, **like** cheaper carpets or anything?
5. ...and I'm **like**, I didn't want to disappoint you...
6. What did it taste **like**?
7. But no, I **like** my work, and there are many unemployed teachers over there.
8. They would **like** some guarantee for the future.
9. ...that can be a problem...when you try to manipulate the hormones **like** that.
10. I would **like** the boys to go and get out their topic folders and colour the map...

11. And the brakes feel **like** they could stop an express train.
12. ...if anyone else would **like** to send anything, it could be put to good use.

11.9 *little*

Little is quite a complicated word. The first distinction that needs to be made is between its use as an adjective, meaning 'small', and its other uses:

> She's a <u>little</u> angel.
> There's <u>little</u> hope left.

In the first example, *little* is an adjective meaning 'small', and *angel* is a singular count noun (hence the use of *a*). In the second example, *little* is a determiner meaning 'a small amount of' or 'not much', and *hope* is a noncount noun.

In this second sense, *little* is also used as a pronoun:

> <u>Little</u> has been done to improve the situation.

and adverb:

> They were <u>little</u> understood.

In these situations, where used on its own, *little* sounds rather formal.

Another dimension that affects *little* is whether it is used with *a* or not. A *little* is regarded as a compound determiner/pronoun/adverb (not as two separate words). Compared to *little* on its own, *a little* has a positive idea, for example:

> There's <u>a</u> <u>little</u> hope left.

Compare this to the second example above.

It is also commonly used with intensifiers:

> There's <u>so</u> <u>little</u> time left.

Activity 11.9a

Decide on these lines whether *little* is:

  a. an adjective
  b. a determiner with noncount nouns
  c. a pronoun
  d. an adverb.

Hint: try replacing *little* with *small/a small amount/to a small extent*.

1. [They] attracted **little** attention as they stepped down the gangplank...
2. ...people are more forgiving for somebody I think if you are a **little** bit late, than if you're too early.
3. ...it's got all the features of an innocent **little** blob.
4. ...underneath his brash exterior there lurks a **little** boy...
5. That's what it says on his **little** card.

6. ...it's all to do with...whether you approve of dressing dogs up in **little** coats...
7. Labour's open hostility to employers will do **little** for business confidence...
8. **Little** fuss has been made of the director 's original notion of casting...
9. ...eventually I suspect it got to be a **little** more organized...
10. ...there's **little** prospect of the government being defeated on it.
11. We have a suspicion that very **little** reaction has taken place...
12. Beat the eggs lightly with a **little** salt and add them to the bowl.
13. ...it is only in this century that we have begun to grow up a **little**.
14. ...the luxuries...did **little** to compensate for her loneliness.
15. The first description seemed a **little** vague to us...

Activity 11.9b

On which lines could *a* be added to change the idea from negative to positive?

11.10 *home*

Home is a very interesting word. While we are all familiar with its basic meaning – 'the place where we live or come from' – there are numerous variations on this meaning associated in part with different grammatical possibilities. It can be:

- a noun, meaning 'the place (in general) where we live':

  We have made a home for ourselves in this community.

  or the actual building people live in:

  A home should be a place where people feel at peace.

  or a special building for a particular group of people:

  She's had to move into a nursing home.

- an adverb indicating location or direction:

  He's still living at home.

  Technically, since it follows a preposition, *home* in this case could be treated as a noun, but it makes more sense to deal with it here as (part of) an adverb phrase. However, if it follows a verb indicating movement, then no preposition is needed:

  They came home to a great celebration.

  (not *to home).

- an adjective, describing something related to where you live – your town or country, as opposed to elsewhere, for example:

  We're looking forward to the home game. (as opposed to an 'away' game)

- a verb:

  The reporters homed in on the unsuspecting stars.

Activity 11.10

Decide on these lines whether *home* is :

a. a noun
b. (part of) an adverb
c. an adjective.

Hint: ask a question beginning *Where...?* to identify the adverb.

1. UK businesses now have a great opportunity in markets both at **home** and abroad...
2. People from the four corners of the world have come to Ontario to make it their **home**.
3. A retirement **home** awaits, in his beloved **home** town...
4. ...it is the **home** climate which gives most concern.
5. It would be cruel if the daughter could be evicted and left to find another **home** for herself...
6. ...when he got **home** he discovered it was the harvest time.
7. My husband and I arrived **home** in Dumfriesshire, after a memorable and highly emotional holiday...
8. ...if you need a lift **home**, just let me know.
9. It is important to judge colour under the conditions you will have at **home**.
10. [He] had been a member of the 99-seat Parliament since he was elected to represent his **home** region...
11. Without it, she has become a virtual prisoner in her own **home**...
12. Then in the morning he thought he'd better be getting back **home** so he started **home**...
13. ...he was schooled in his **home** town before studying chemistry at Liverpool University.
14. At **home** Scotch Whisky is a drink for all occasions...
15. ...we hope to gain a better understanding of how the different elements of a **home** worked.
16. Phosphates are also present in detergents and cleaners used in the **home**.

Chapter 12

Multi-functional words (II)

12.0 Introduction

This chapter, like Chapter 11, deals with words that belong to a number of word classes but, in this case, there is a slight difference. All the word classes that they belong to are functional and closed in nature rather than open: word classes such as pronoun and determiner (Chapter 3) and prepositions (Chapter 5), not to mention personal pronouns (Chapter 2). Also included are adverbs (Chapter 6) and conjunctions (see below), which are traditionally recognised as content/open word classes. However, they do not admit new members as freely as the central open and content word classes: nouns, adjectives and verbs.

A number of words in this chapter belong to the word class 'conjunction', which has not been described before. Conjunctions are words that join two **clauses** together. There are two types: 'coordinating conjunctions', namely *and*, *but* and *or*, which join two equal clauses together:

I like her __and__ she likes me.

and subordinating conjunctions, which place a subordinate clause inside another:

I like her __because__ she likes me.

In this respect they are similar to subordinators, which are dealt with in Chapter 10 with one major exception: *that*, which is dealt with below.

Because they join two ideas in the same sentence, conjunctions cover some of the same meanings as linking adverbs (see Chapter 6), but they link the ideas more closely:

We let them in __even though__ they were late. (conjunction)
They were late. __Nevertheless__, we let them in. (linking adverb)

12.1 *that*

According to most frequency lists, *that* is the seventh most frequent word in English. It is a very versatile word (some would say 'confusing') in that it can appear in several roles. First, it can appear in a number of word classes:

- demonstrative pronoun. In this situation, *that* functions as the equivalent of noun phrases:

I like __that__. / __That__ won't work.

It has the idea of something distant from the speaker, as opposed to *this*.

- demonstrative determiner. In this use *that* is part of a noun phrase:

I like *that idea*. / *That idea* won't work.

- adverb. Here, *that* is a degree adverb (or intensifier) modifying another adjective or adverb:

I tell you, it was *that big*.

In this respect it can be regarded as an informal equivalent of *so*.

Activity 12.1a

Identify on the lines below where *that* is a:

a. demonstrative pronoun
b. demonstrative determiner
c. degree adverb.

Hint: work out the word class of the word following *that*.

1. I wasn't expecting you'd be **that** busy just now.
2. I shouldn't have laid **that** carpet last night.
3. In the past month in here, well, it's been like **that** every day.
4. …Kahn moved into **that** field from the excellent springboard of general practice.
5. Will you please remember to do **that** for me?
6. And 40 years ago **that** is just what Peter Conder… set out to do.
7. He probably told you **that** just to explain things.
8. There you are young Walter, and **that**'ll keep you for a week.
9. You will be entitled to remove any growing plants within **that** period.
10. …we shall not come to take a reading **that** quarter.
11. Oh dear, **that**'s a shame.
12. Too many pockets, **that**'s what the trouble is.

Although the first two uses of *that* above are the most basic ones (and are the first ones presented to learners), they are not the most common. By far the most common use of *that* is to introduce a wide range of clauses:

- relative clauses (as a relative pronoun). Again it is versatile in this role, and can replace most other relative pronouns, whether as **subject** or **object**, whether human or non-human:

She is a person *that* knows how to handle herself. (subject, human)
She is a person *that* we can trust. (object, human)
This was the argument *that* proved conclusive. (subject, non-human)
This was an argument *that* we couldn't refute. (object, non-human)

When it represents the object it can be omitted:

She is a person we can trust.

There are some restrictions here on the use of *that*; it cannot occur in **non-defining** or **sentential** relative clauses:

*I met my sister, that had been waiting for me. (should be ...*who*...)
*Then she relaxed, that made everyone happy. (should be ...*which*...)

- nominal clauses, as subject, object (most common) and **predicative**:

That he is only 25 doesn't bother me. (subject)
Everyone knows that we are broke. *(object)*
The problem is that we can't find anyone to replace her. (predicative)

That also appears in cases of **extraposition**, when a nominal clause (usually a subject but also an object) is 'extraposed' to the end of the sentence and replaced by *it*:

It is obvious that he was murdered.

(cf. *That he was murdered is obvious*.)

- complement clauses. Here, *that* and its accompanying clause completes the meaning of the adjective or noun preceding it:

I'm glad that you're friends again.
There's a feeling that we should cancel the meeting.

In a sense the complement acts as the 'object' of the adjective or noun (cf. 'we feel that we should cancel...').

- appositive clauses. Here, the clause introduced by *that* stands in a one-to-one relationship ('apposition') with the preceding noun phrase, and if either is omitted the sentence still makes grammatical sense:

The idea that we should give up is ridiculous. ('The idea is ridiculous.'/ 'That we should give up is ridiculous.')

- adverbial clauses of purpose (answering the question *why*) when preceded by *so*:

We put it in writing so that there could be no argument later.

In the last four cases, *that* is sometimes called a 'subordinator. (Other subordinators are explained in Chapter 10.) *That* can be deleted (except when it introduces a subject nominal clause):

Everyone knows we are broke.

Activity 12.1b

Identify the function of *that* on these concordance lines according to the uses described above. Decide whether it:

a. is a relative pronoun
b. introduces a nominal clause
c. is a case of extraposition
d. introduces a complement clause
e. introduces an appositive clause
f. is part of *so that*.

Hint: test for relative pronoun *that* by replacing it with *which* or *who*.

1. They are, personally, bearing all the costs of the ride so **that** all monies raised will benefit the Fund.
2. Both will keep down our costs – costs **that** are reflected in the price you pay for electricity.
3. On 28 May we informed the company **that**, inadvertently, we omitted the following paragraph from our Report...
4. ...we consider **that** it is appropriate that further development should take place in the village...
5. ...I understand **that** it may be of interest to your wife's mother.
6. What happened was **that** it was the son...
7. ...now I've still got this sore tongue **that** keeps coming back, very badly.
8. This week's figures suggest **that** one in three motorists are buying unleaded...
9. She didn't bother to tell me **that** she'd only got to call you, right?
10. There are a variety of reasons for a belief **that** structural adjustments to the EC budget are not over.
11. It has become clear **that** the anti-vivisection movement is now far better organised and directed than in the past.
12. A lot of my friends are pleased **that** the company is doing the job they are doing.
13. Trips to Ireland recently have reinforced my view **that** the P (probationer) plate... is a good thing and should be adopted here.
14. Overseas members are asked to ensure **that** their remittance is in the form of a sterling draft...
15. The RDS is fighting to resist the effect **that** these campaigns are having on public opinion.
16. We are improving the network of routes our meter readers follow, so **that** we use the most efficient and economic pattern of working.
17. All of our reparation work is based on the fact **that** we want people to volunteer to do this work.
18. Dr Cuzick said it was very likely **that** women with only minor abnormalities but high levels of HPV 16 might well have high grade disease...

Activity 12.1c

Decide on the lines above in Activity 12.1b whether *that* can be omitted.

12.2 *there*

There is used in two main ways: as an adverb of place meaning 'in that place', and as a way of introducing 'existential' sentences:

> <u>There</u> *are many ways to catch a rat.*

Here, *there* is not pointing to any particular place; it is simply stating the existence of 'many ways…'. It is a way of avoiding a clumsy construction with the verb *be* (**Many ways are to catch a rat.*) It is easy to see that these two uses are different as they can both occur in the same sentence:

> <u>There</u> *were several protesters* <u>there</u> *in the hall already.*

Existential *there* is used typically with forms of the verb *be*, often contracted (e.g. *there's*), though other verbs, such as *seem*, *appear* and *exist*, are possible. It occurs clause-initially, in the subject position preceding the verb, but the verb itself agrees with the following noun phrase ('several protesters' in the example above). In informal English a singular verb may be followed by a plural noun phrase:

> <u>There's</u> <u>several people</u> *waiting to see you.*

Adverb *there* can also be clause-initial and stressed: <u>There</u> *she is.* Note that there is a subject following it. There are also a number of idiomatic uses of adverb *there* to look out for: *there you go/so there/there, there.* Check these in a good dictionary.

Activity 12.2

Decide whether the following lines have:

>   a. existential *there*
>   b. adverb *there*

Hint: not all cases where *there* comes at the start of a clause are existential.

>   1. It is easy to see that **there** are 12 pentagons on the ball.
>   2. **There** she found a spring.
>   3. A spokesman … denied **there** was a risk to people in offices or homes.
>   4. How do you remain calm when **there**'re all these things?
>   5. …[he] has often returned **there** to keep fresh the memory…
>   6. …**there** is also the satisfaction of learning new skills…
>   7. …**there** was no way of knowing which women were in that group.
>   8. **There** you are, young man.
>   9. They will be **there** to explain the plan…
>   10. …**there** seems to be no 'convenient point of entry'.

12.3 *one*

One is the 39th most frequent word in English according to one frequency count. It is usually thought of as the first cardinal number: *one, two, three*, etc. But while it is common in this respect, it is also commonly used as a pronoun in a number of ways:

- as a formal personal pronoun for making generalisations:

One has to get on with one's life.

- as a substitute pronoun for nouns to avoid repetition:

You take the blue case and I'll take the black one. (= 'case')

- as an indefinite pronoun, referring back to indefinite noun phrases:

Just because you want a car, it doesn't mean you get one. (= 'a car')

Notice how in the last example *one* replaces the whole noun phrase, whereas in the previous use it only replaces the noun. In all three cases it does not have the idea of a number; it would be strange or impossible to replace it with *two*.

Another situation where *one* does not have the idea of a number is when it is part of a time adverbial:

One day you'll see I was right.

Activity 12.3

On these lines decide whether one is:

a. a numeral
b. a formal personal pronoun
c. a substitute pronoun
d. part of a time adverbial.

Hint: try replacing *one* with *two* (and changing the form of the noun and verb if necessary).

1. Inside, **one** can still see the Map Room…
2. …he seems the only **one** capable of communicating sanely…
3. But **one** day a magician accidentally spilt silver dust all over them…
4. The last **one** I got is not in there.
5. …you take the first **one** immediately before you go to bed…
6. Even if you only buy **one** in a whole year, we will still be happy to give you all the benefits…
7. If you want to try those, you dissolve **one** in four litres of water…
8. We looked at the gains and losses…associated with the process of detachment from **one** job and attachment to another.
9. There are some changes which **one** might have expected…
10. **One** morning Polly looked at her privet bush and sighed.
11. What happens if they went **one** nil up?
12. Let's assume **one** of your employees drinks too much both at work and at home.
13. Story-reading should be **one** of the great joys of parenthood…
14. …membership is available at a subscription of **one** pound per annum…
15. I suppose that's a good thing in **one** way.

12.4 *no*

No is one of the 50 most frequent words in English, as a result of the several different ways in which it is used. It can be:

- a determiner with all types of noun:

  I have <u>no</u> idea. (count singular)
  I have <u>no</u> ideas. (count plural)
  We have <u>no</u> hope. (noncount)

  Compared to *no, not any* tends to be less emphatic:

  We haven't <u>any</u> hope.

  It is also found in notices containing prohibitions:

  NO SMOKING

- an adverb with comparatives and *different*:

  Tomorrow's weather will be <u>no</u> better/different.

- in answers

  Can I go out? – <u>No</u>.

  This is the commonest use.

Unlike most determiners, *no* is not used as a pronoun; *none* may be considered a pronoun equivalent:

  When we got there, there were <u>no tables</u>/<u>none</u> left.

Activity 12.4

Decide whether *no* on these lines is:

  a. a determiner with a singular count noun
  b. a determiner with a plural count noun
  c. a determiner with a noncount noun
  d. an answer
  e. an adverb.

Hint: where appropriate try replacing *no* with *not* and *a/an* to find out what type of noun follows.

1. **No** correspondence will be entered into.
2. ...there has, to our knowledge, been **no** detailed study...
3. ...the poet tells him there is **no** paradise and **no** hell...
4. **No**, he got stuck in London the night before because of the bad weather.
5. [...there are] young people who can see **no** likelihood of ever finding meaningful employment.

6. My daughter thought **no** more of it...
7. **No** previous knowledge is required for a five-day course on Conservation.
8. The world has **no** reason to doubt that this entente is based on a genuine personal chemistry...
9. There is **no** scientific data to substantiate this hypothesis.
10. ...the two-tier minimum spirits rate makes **no** sense...
11. I just send it in, there'll be **no** problem then. – **No** problem.
12. **No** wonder you're not hearing so good.

12.5 *enough*

Enough is used:

- as a determiner with plural count nouns and noncount nouns meaning 'sufficient':

  All we need is to get <u>enough signatures</u>.
  There's been <u>enough rain</u> for a month.

- as a pronoun:

  I've got plenty of food; have you got <u>enough</u>?

- as an adverb postmodifying adjectives and adverbs, meaning 'sufficiently':

  They're <u>happy enough</u> with the new flat.

  Note its position after the adjective.

- as an adjective:

  For some people wealth is not <u>enough</u>.

As an adverb it is often used with **comment adverbs**:

  <u>Interestingly enough</u>, nobody noticed the mistake.

Activity 12.5

Work out whether *enough* on the lines below is:

a. an adverb postmodifying adjectives and adverbs (one of which is a comment adverb)
b. a determiner
c. a pronoun
d. an adjective.

Hint: try replacing *enough* with *sufficient(ly)*, changing the word order if necessary.

1. ...teachers' views...are not taken seriously **enough** by the decision makers...
2. Keeping the law is not **enough**.
3. ...we have large stocks of coal in this country, **enough** for about two hundred years...
4. They're not good **enough** for the British people.
5. ...farmers did not...lobby hard **enough** for their interests...

6. The basic claim of the Principle is plausible **enough**...
7. Is that beef cooked **enough**?
8. Wesker wrote that all he wanted was **enough** money to give the play a chance.
9. ...are there **enough** officers on duty to prevent more violence?
10. 'Cos I haven't got **enough**.
11. And strangely **enough** she felt that she knew him...
12. There was just **enough** time for a picnic...
13. The game plan is to grow big **enough** to threaten even the city giants.
14. ...some people have been unkind **enough** to suggest that it was but recently invented...
15. Our only hope is that **enough** toys are produced...

12.6 *so*

So is a very versatile word. It can be used as:

- a linking adverb:

  The light was getting bad. So we had to abandon the search.

- a conjunction:

  The light was getting bad so we had to abandon the search.
  There is little difference in meaning between this and the previous example; the conjunction brings the two ideas closer together.

- a degree adverb (intensifier):

  It's so hot today.

- a 'proform', where it takes the place of an element for the sake of brevity:

  Can I have some biscuits? I don't think so. (= *I don't think you can have some biscuits*)

Recently, *so* has been acquiring a meaning as a modal adverb:

  I'm so not getting this. (= 'really', 'definitely')

It also occurs in a number of expressions or constructions: *and so on, or so* (= 'roughly') and *so...as, so...that* (see 12.1).

Activity 12.6

Identify on the following lines where *so* is:

a. a linking adverb
b. a degree adverb (intensifer)
c. a proform
d. part of a construction or expression. (NB. the other part of the expression may be separated from *so* by several words.)

Hint: is something earlier implied?

1. **So** does that sound okay to you?
2. **So** I think we ought to have a chat about the sort of things he's putting you on…
3. **So** it's actually all about what the English did…
4. **So** it's not an easy life?
5. Shakespeare does not **so** much take sides as show how the state is threatened…
6. Why was **so** much noise and trouble caused over the poll tax?
7. I'm **so** new to the area…
8. …you would forget about him straight away because it's **so** obvious.
9. The economy has been **so** strong in the last few years…
10. I'm not **so** sure about that.
11. **So** that I take it there's a lot of work to do…
12. Pardon me for saying **so**, that's a lovely pen.
13. [He] has the priceless gift of making the language tangible **so** that when he says 'I think he'll be to Rome as is the osprey to the fish' the image comes resonantly alive.
14. Right, well **so** he's done that has he? Well I imagine **so**…
15. **So** you're better out the way of that for a week or **so**.

12.7 *as*

As is a very versatile word. It can be a preposition meaning 'in the capacity/function of':

> She worked <u>as</u> a teacher for many years.

It can be a subordinating conjunction with a number of meanings:

- reason (similar to *since*): As you didn't call, I assumed you weren't coming.
- time: <u>As</u> winter approaches, birds start to circle.
- manner: We enjoyed it, <u>as</u> most people did.

In this case there may be **inversion**:

> We enjoyed it, <u>as</u> <u>did</u> <u>most people</u>. (as most people did)

It is also commonly used in pairs as a degree adverb to indicate two things that are being compared – the first an adjective, the second a noun phrase:

> We're <u>as</u> happy <u>as</u> children in a sweet-shop.

In addition it is often used in expressions with other words:

- *as if, as though, as long as, as soon as* as conjunctions;
- *such as* to indicate examples;
- *as well, as well as* to indicate something added.

Activity 12.7

Identify on these lines whether *as* is:

a. a preposition
b. a conjunction, and of which sort (reason, time, manner)

c.   part of *as...as*

d.   part of an expression with another word (or words).

Note: only one example of *as* per line is highlighted; to find a second *as* you may have to look some distance.

Hint: look at the words following *as*; you may have to look quite far.

1.   Lorna has been active **as** a tenants' leader...
2.   [It] will also be available **as** an up-to-date slide set...
3.   [They] are arguably **as** vital a part of the educational process as any learning about text.
4.   For **as** little as £2 per month [it] will be mailed to your home every week.
5.   ...preliminary research suggested crops such **as** barley, peas, cauliflower, sprouts and broccoli were most at risk.
6.   Otherwise she's **as** cheery as ever.
7.   [It] could cause serious damage to crops...**as** extra ultra-violet radiation reaches the planet's surface.
8.   He has done his best, **as** have other surgeons and doctors at the hospital...
9.   **As** I said, we may not have a set-up...
10. Observers saw Mrs Thatcher's comments **as** little more than the latest in a series of delaying tactics.
11. **As** part of her study, she asked children to draw pictures of their family...
12. It could be something **as** simple as that...
13. And **as** the nappies are thinner, there's 30% less waste.
14. Well, **as** soon as the doctor mentioned hospital, she was awfully upset.
15. However, things are not **as** bad as they seem.
16. ...you will find the time to study our in-depth campaign reports **as** they become available.
17. ...it looked for a long time **as** though that was going to be the only goal...
18. I've got a sore back **as** well.
19. Its dense growth provides nesting places for a range of bird life **as** well as warm cover in winter for roosting small birds.
20. Her situation is desperately serious, **as** is also the situation of the unborn child.

12.8 *before*

Before is used in a number of ways:

- as a subordinating conjunction:

   Don't forget to say 'goodbye' before you go.

- as a preposition referring to time:

   We must leave before ten.

   as well as to position (= 'in front of'):

   What you see before you is the next big thing.

- as an adverb (= 'beforehand'):

I've seen her <u>before</u>.

Activity 12.8

Decide whether *before* on the lines is:

a. a conjunction
b. a preposition (and whether it refers to time or place)
c. an adverb.

Hint: look at what follows *before*.

1. **Before** a questioning audience Mr Murray began by explaining the main features…
2. …the hearing…would require to be heard **before** at least two judges.
3. Crops of corn and vegetables were cultivated, along with many herbs and plants not known in Britain **before**.
4. [They] believe that there has to be an agreement **before** December the fifteenth…
5. A warm drink **before** going to bed may help to keep you warm.
6. And we have done this **before**, haven't we?
7. …he was vicar from 1964 until his death, five days **before** he was due to retire.
8. animals and other creatures were around a long time **before** human beings…
9. And it ripped about a quarter of the roof off **before** it finished…
10. I think we should join well **before** next summer…
11. Naturally it was not long **before** other brewers saw the potential…
12. [He] believes interest rates will drop by a full 1pc **before** the end of the year…
13. It is not enough that hedges are…greener yesterday than they were the day **before**.
14. …something was going on…a few months **before** the book was published!
15. [It] had been hidden since **before** the First World War.

12.9 *since*

Since is used in a number of ways. It can be:

- a subordinating conjunction denoting a relationship of time or reason:

We've known him <u>since</u> he was small. (time)
<u>Since</u> you ask, I've spent it. (reason)

- a time preposition:

We've lived here <u>since</u> 2010.

- an adverb referring to an already-specified point in time:

And ever <u>since</u>, no one's asked about it.

Activity 12.9

Decide whether *since* on these lines is:

a. a conjunction (and whether it refers to time or reason)
b. a preposition
c. an adverb.

Hint: look at the words that come after *since*.

1. [They] have taken part in almost every ceremonial occasion in Scotland **since** 1946.
2. [This] has been evidenced by what has happened **since**.
3. It also matters currently, **since** art is to be included as a foundation subject...
4. Thirty years **since** Asterix came to life, sales of the books so far have topped 180 million...
5. But **since** his arrival at the theatre five years ago he has worked with the artistic director...
6. I really wanted to study French at university, **since** I was interested in languages.
7. I haven't put on any weight **since** I gave up dieting!
8. **Since** last summer at least 256 teachers had lost their jobs...
9. Been a long time **since** she had heard her language spoken freely.
10. ...he has prepared a batch every November **since**.
11. ...**since** the turn of the 20th century it has become the company's major product.
12. ...money has been coming in much quicker **since** then.
13. And **since** they've refused repeatedly to have a public inquiry...we're not certain of the safety of what's coming out.
14. Drivers themselves cannot take the initiative **since** they can do nothing to relieve towns and cities...
15. ...**since** this is a relatively new area...we felt it our responsibility to report this.

Answers

Chapter 1 – Nouns

Activity 1.1

a. count: 2, 4 and 6
b. noncount: 1, 3, 5, 7, 8 and 9. This reflects the predominance of the noncount use.

On line 10, *wood* is a premodifier, not the head of the noun phrase, and so the count/noncount distinction is not so relevant. However, the meaning referred to is clearly the count one: a collection of trees (it is not a pigeon made of wood).

Activity 1.2

a. count: lines 1, 5, 6, 7, 8 and 9
b. noncount: 2, 3, 4 and 10

Activity 1.3

a. count: 1, 3, 6, 8 and 10
b. noncount: 2, 5, 7 and 9. On line 4 it is a premodifier; the count/nouncount distinction is not so relevant here (though the meaning is the noncount one).

Activity 1.4

a. count: 2 and 6
b. noncount: 1, 3, 5, 7, 8, 9 and 10. On line 4 it is a premodifier; on line 9 it refers to a body of artistic works.

Activity 1.5

a. count: lines 1, 2, 4, 6 and 7
b. noncount: lines 3, 5 and 8

Activity 1.6

a. count: 7, 8 and 10
b. noncount ('universe'): 1, 2 and 4 (in 4 it is a premodifier)
c. noncount ('empty area'): 3, 5, 6 and 9

Activity 1.7

On line 3 *room* is noncount. On all the others it is count, including line 5, where *the* has been deleted because it is in parallel with *chimney* (*between the chimney and the room* is also possible).

Activity 1.8

On lines 3, 5 and 10 *arms* is a noncount noun referring to weapons. In all three cases it is a premodifier.

Activity 1.9

Customs is the plural of a count noun on lines 3, 6, 8 and 10. On the other lines it is a plural noun. Of these, on lines 1, 2, 5 and 7 it is a premodifier of a following head noun.

Activity 1.10

a. singular agreement: 4 and 8
b. plural agreement: 1, 2, 5 and 9
c. not certain: 3, 6, 7 and 10

Activity 1.11

a. single body: 5, 6, 8 and 9
b. collection of individuals: 1 and 4
c. not clear: 2, 3, 7 and 10. However, on lines 3 and 10 *committee* could only be regarded as a single unit, and on line 2 there is a subsequent *its*.

Chapter 2 – Personal pronouns

Activity 2.1

a. referring to people in general: 7 and 9
b. referring to specific listeners or readers: 1, 2, 3 (both cases), 4, 5, 6 (second case), 8 and 10.
c. a determiner: 6 (first case)

Activity 2.2

a. exclusive: 1, 2, 3, 5, 7, 8 and 9. This is evident on lines 1, 2, 3, 5 and 9 because of the opposition to *you, your* or *everyone*. On lines 7 and 8 new information is being given to addressees.

b. inclusive: 6 (clearly, because of *together*) and 10 (probably, because it sounds like an attempt to involve the reader).

Line 4 could be either: the presenters of a show exclusively, or them plus the audience inclusively (probably the latter).

On lines 2 and 5 *we* is referring back to 'The Council' and 'The Trust' respectively.

Activity 2.3

1. *rained consultants*
2. *corals*
3. *marine engines*
4. *Popes*
5. There is no referent in this text. *They* is referring to an unspecified group of people, presumably experts in the field.
6. *the defendants*
7. *your casualty*. The reference is to a singular noun phrase and *he or she* could be used. Here, *your* is being used generically (see Section 2.2).
8. *interviewees*
9. *his biggest decisions*
10. *most people*

Activity 2.4

a. possessive determiner: 1, 2 and 6
b. objective pronoun: 3, 4 and 5

Activity 2.5

a. emphatic: 1, 5, 6 and 7
b. reflexive: 2, 3, 4, 9, 10 and 11
c. alternative to *me*: 8 and 12

Activity 2.6

a. On the following lines *it* is referring back to the following noun phrases:

3. *too much phosphorus*
4. *Transcendental Meditation*
5. *Parasitology* (the name of a Journal)
8. *The well*
9. *the dirt on fabrics*
10. *the harmless bat*
11. *the enclosed Proceedings Order Form*
12. *the railway*
16. *his business*

17. *your car*
19. *The equipment supplied*
20. *any pack*

b. anticipatory subject: lines 1, 13, 15 and 18. Apart from line 1 where one could say *Does to swallow hurt?* (though *Does swallowing hurt?* is better) the lines would be very clumsy without anticipatory *it*, e.g. for 18:

> But that I know their candidates' attitudes before deciding remains essential.

There are no lines where it is an anticipatory object.

c. general circumstances: lines 2, 6, 14. On line 3 we could regard *it* as referring back to the whole of the preceding clause: '*if...rivers*'.
expression: line 7 (*take my word for it* = 'trust me')

Chapter 3 – Pronouns and determiners

Activity 3.1

a. determiner: 9, 14 and 15
   pronoun: 8, 12 and 13
   adverb: 1, 2, 3, 4, 5, 6, 7, 10 and 11
b. On the following lines *much* may sound formal, with potential replacements in brackets: 1 (*greatly*), 5 (*greatly*), 12 (*a lot of*), 13 (*a lot*) and 14 (*a lot of*).
c. *Much* is preceded by an intensifier on lines 2, 3, 6, 7, 8, 9, 10 and 15 (and therefore does not sound formal). On all of them it would sound strange or incorrect if the intensifier was removed, except for lines 2 and 7, because these are non-assertive contexts; both are negative.

Activity 3.2

a. On lines 6, 9, 10, 13 and 15 *many* is a pronoun; on all the other lines it is a determiner.
b. *Many* is modified by the intensifiers *too* (line 2), *so* (3), *very* (11) and *how* (12 and 15)
c. *Many* precedes *a* on line 1 (forming a compound determiner) and follows *all our* on line 4.

Activity 3.3a

a. comparative: 2, 3, 4, 5, 6, 7 and 14
b. determiner: 1, 9 and 10
c. adverb alone: 8 and 15
d. expression: 12
e. pronoun: 11 and 13

On line 4 *more* could possibly be interpreted as a determiner ('a greater amount of difficult wastes') rather than a comparative ('wastes that are more difficult').

Activity 3.3b

While *much* as an adverb modifies *more* as an adverb, which in turn modifies *complicated* to form a comparative adjective, *many* in this situation has two possible interpretations. It could be a determiner preceding a comparative ('many issues which are more complicated'), or it could be an adverb modifying the determiner *more*, while *complicated* is an adjective ('many more issues which are complicated').

Activity 3.4

a. part of a superlative adjective or adverb: 4, 5, 6, 8, 12, 14 and (probably) 15
b. intensifier: 7, 13 and possibly 15.
c. determiner: 2, 3, 11 (an expression: *for the most part*)
d. pronoun: 1, 9, 10

As regards line 15, the probable interpretation is that landfill is the most suitable solution out of all solutions.

Activity 3.5

a. a determiner with plural count nouns: 3, 4, 8, 11, 13 and 15
b. a determiner with noncount nouns: 7, 9 and 12
c. a determiner with singular count nouns: 2, 5 and 14. (In 14 *some* implies a rather large amount.)
d. a pronoun: 6 and 10
e. an adverb: 1

Activity 3.6

a. On the following lines, *any* + a negative is non-assertive because it can be replaced by *no/ none:*... : 1 (*But they grow no sweeter*...), 2, 3, 6, 8, 9, 10, 11, 13 and 15
   On the following lines it cannot be replaced: 4, 5, 7, 12 and 14
b. adverb: 1 and 8
   pronoun: 15
   determiner: 2, 3, 4, 5, 6, 7, 9, 10, 11, 12, 13 and 14. All these lines have a singular count noun, apart from 10 and 11 (plural count noun) and 9 and 14 (noncount noun).

Activity 3.7

a. a determiner modifying count nouns: 2 and 10 (In both cases *fewer* could replace *less* because the head nouns, *issues* and *people*, are count plural.)
b. a determiner modifying noncount nouns: 5, 9, 11 (both cases) and 14
c. an adverb modifying adjectives and adverbs: 3, 4, 6, 7 and 12
d. an adverb: 8
e. a pronoun: 15
f. an expression: 1 and 13

Activity 3.8

a. central determiner: 9 and 12
b. predeterminer: 10, 11 and 13
c. delayed determiner: 2, 3, 5 and 15
d. pronoun: 7, 8 and 14
e. adverb: 4
f. part of an expression: 1 (*at all*) and 6 (*all of a sudden* = 'suddenly')

Activity 3.9

a. a central determiner: 1, 4, 5, 10 and 11
b. a predeterminer: 13
c. a pronoun: 2, 3, 6, 7, 9 and 15
d. a coordinator with *and*: 8 and 14
e. a delayed determiner: 12

Activity 3.10

a. abstract noun: 4, 5 and 6
b. time period: 1 and 7
c. part of a conjunction: 12 (*every time that…*)
d. not followed by a noun: lines 8 (an expression) and 9 (*every one*)

On lines 2, 3, 10 and 11 it is followed by a non-abstract count noun.

Activity 3.11

a. pronoun: lines 1, 5 and 9
   determiner: all the other lines.
b. most of the lines already have *a few* (or *the few*). On line 1 to add *a* would be very strange because it would contradict the first part of the sentence; on lines 6 and 7 it could be added.

Chapter 4 – Adjectives

Comment 4.1

Brave is both an attributive adjective (lines 2, 3, 4, 5, 6, 11 and 12) and predicative adjective (lines 7, 8, 9 and 10; note the use of *feel* as a link verb on line 7, instead of *be*, and the fronting on line 8, whereby *brave* is placed at the start of the sentence). On line 1 it is the head of a noun phrase (along with another adjective, *strong*). It is also gradable (lines 2, 6 and 7).

Comment 4.2

Homeless is used attributively (lines 5, 7, 8 and 10) and predicatively (lines 1, 2 and 4), and as the head of a noun phrase with generic reference (3, 6 and 9). It is not gradable.

Comment 4.3

Poor is used mainly as an attributive adjective (all lines except 9, 14 and 15). On lines 14 and 15 it is used predicatively, while on line 9 it is the head of a noun phrase. It is gradable (lines 12 and 13).

As far as meanings are concerned, the attributive use has a wide range including, 'low in quality' (lines 2, 3, 4, 5, 11, 12 and 13), 'unfortunate' (referring to people, lines 6, 8 and 10) and 'lacking money' (lines 1 and 7). These meanings also apply to the predicative uses, but as head of a noun phrase it can only mean 'people lacking money'.

Comment 4.4

Mere is only used as an attributive adjective. (Note the use of *a mere* in front of numbers on line 1, 2 and 3.) It is not gradable.

Comment 4.5

Former is only used attributively (all the lines except 5), not predicatively. On line 5 it is the head of the noun phrase, with the meaning 'not the latter'. It also has this meaning on line 1. On all the other lines it refers to something that used to be. It is not gradable.

Comment 4.6

Ill is a predicative adjective on the majority of the lines: 1, 4, 5, 7, 10, 12, 13, 14 and 15. However, there are clear cases where *ill* premodifies various nouns as an attributive adjective: *effects* on line 6, *health* on lines 8 and 9, *patients* on line 11, and one perhaps not so clear: *people* on line 2. So it is not true to say *ill* is not used attributively, but there are clearly limitations on its use as such.

On line 3 it is the head of the noun phrase, referring generically (and modified by the adverb *mentally*; without this it would sound strange). It is gradable, as lines 7, 10, 14 and 15 demonstrate.

Comment 4.7

Ready is almost always followed by an adjective complement. The two types are a prepositional phrase beginning with *for* (lines 1 to 5) and a *to* infinitive (lines 7 to 10). There are also three lines (6, 11 and 12) where there is no complement.

Comment 4.8

There are two types of adjective complement with *happy*: prepositional phrases starting with *about* (line 1) and *with* (8 and 9), and *to* infinitives (4, 5, 6 and 7). Another type of complement, a *that*-clause is not represented in the lines.

On two lines (3 and 10) *happy* is used predicatively but with no complement. On one line (2) it is an attributive adjective. On lines 7, 9 and 10 it is preceded by an intensifier.

Comment 4.9

As the lines show, *fond* is quite common as an attributive adjective (lines 1, 2, 3, 11 and 12). When it is used predicatively it is always followed by a prepositional phrase starting with *of* as a complement.

Comment 4.10

a. On lines 2 to 8, *aware* is a predicative adjective followed by a complement consisting of a prepositional phrase starting with *of*. On lines 9, 10 and 11 the complement is a *that-*clause. On line 1, while it is predicative, there is no complement.
b. On line 12 it is used attributively.

Comment 4.11

a. *Late* is attributive on lines 1, 2, 4 and 10.
b. On lines 1 and 4 (referring to a latter period) and line 10 (meaning 'dead') its meaning only applies attributively.
c. On lines 3, 5, 6 and 7 it is an adverb.

On lines 8 and 9 it is a predicative adjective.

Comment 4.12

a. *Old* is attributive on lines 3, 4 5, 6 and 7.
b. On lines 3 (probably) and 7 (definitely) it indicates affection.
c. On line 8 it is a generic adjective referring to old people as the head of the noun phrase.

On lines 1 and 2 it is a predicative adjective.

Activity 4.13

a. predicative adjective: 2, 3, 4, 5, 6 and 7. (There are no examples of an attributive adjective, though it is possible: *satisfied customers*.)
b. *-ed* participle: 1 and 8, where it is part of a passive.

Two types of adjective complement are shown: *satisfied* <u>with</u>... (lines 4, 5, 6 and 7) and *satisfied* <u>that</u>... (lines 2 and 3, although *that* is omitted in 3).

Activity 4.14

a. attributive: 3, 4, 10 and 12
b. predicative: 1, 2, 5, 6, 7, 8 and 9 (On lines 2 and 9 it represents the object predicative rather than subject predicative.)
c. *-ing* participle: line 11

A number of degree adverbs are used to modify *amusing*: *so* (line 1), *very* (3, 5 and 12), *quite* (7), *how* (8) and *highly* (9).

Chapter 5 – Prepositions

Activity 5.1a

Replacing *of* with a genitive:

a. is possible: 2 (*the recording centre's industry*), 3 (*the diesel boom's demands*), 5 (*the first-person speaker's identity*), 7 (*the teacher's primary function*), 8 (*the clans' more dominant member*), 10 (*drama and literature's turn*) and 11 (*the tumour's growth*)
b. sounds strange: 1 (*?the book's course*), 6 (*?the tuition fees' level*)
c. makes no sense: 4, 9 (but *a very general reference point* is possible) and 12

Note: since intuitions are involved, not everyone will agree with the above answers.

Activity 5.1b

a. part of a quantifying expression: 4 (first example), 6, 11
b. means 'consist of': 5 (both examples), 10, 12, 15, 17 and 18
c. part of a prepositional verb: 1, 13 and 14 ('accuse someone of...')
d. part of an expression or multi-word preposition: 3 (*out of*), 4 (first example – *because of*) and 8 (*in the event of*)
e. indicates an underlying verbal relationship (verb + object): 7 ('they discussed...'), 9 ('they remembered...') and 16 (all three examples)
f. part of an adjective complement: 2

Activity 5.2a

a. necessitated by preceding semi-modals: 1, 12, 14 and 19
b. necessitated by a preceding adjective or noun to introduce a complement: 4, 7, 8 (second example) and 11. Line 1 also contains an adjective (*able*), but this is best regarded as part of a semi-modal.
c. necessitated by a preceding main verb: 6, 17 and 20

Activity 5.2b

a. introduces a prepositional complement after a noun or adjective: 10, 13 and 15
b. is part of a prepositional verb: 3 and 9
c. introduces an adverbial: 5, 8 (first example) and 16
d. introduces a prepositional object: 18
e. is part of a multi-word preposition: 2

Activity 5.3

a. adverbial of place: 2, 4, 5, 7, 9, 11 and 12 (first example)
b. adverbial of time: 8
c. adverbial of manner: 1 and 10
d. expression: 6, 12 (second example)
e. phrasal verb: 3 (*book in*; note the passive idea)

Activity 5.4

a. adverbial indicating date: 2, 5, 10 and 11 (could also be b)
b. adverbial indicating location: 1, 6 and 11 (could also be a)
c. part of a noun complement: 7, 8, 9 and 12
d. part of a prepositional verb: 3 and 4. (Actually in 3 it is part of a phrasal-prepositional verb *cut down on*)

Activity 5.5

a. adverbial of duration: 1, 11 and 12
b. adverbial of reason: 2 and 14
c. adverbial indicating a beneficiary: 4, 8 and 9
d. adverbial indicating a representative: 10
e. noun or adjective complement: 3, 6 and 7
f. prepositional verb: 5 and 13

Activity 5.6

a. an agent following a passive: 1, 5, 8, 10 and 11
b. a non-passive agent: 3, 6, 7 and 9
c. the creator of a work: 2 (the second example), 12 and 15
d. an adverbial of place: 2 (the first example)
   an adverbial of manner: 4 and 13 (answering the question *How...?*) and 14 (*How much...?*)

Activity 5.7

a. adverbial of time: 1 and 6
b. adverbial of place: 2, 3 (both instances), 5 (both instances), 7, 8 and 10

The remaining lines are line 4, where *at* is part of a prepositional verb *look at*, and line 9, where it is part of the expression *at all*.

Chapter 6 – Adverbs

Activity 6.1

a. aspect adverb: 1, 2, 3, 4, 5, 6, 8, 10 and 11 (all in middle position)
b. linking adverb: 7
c. degree adverb: 9 (modifying the comparative 'nearer')
d. adjective: 12. This sentence is a proverb.

Activity 6.2

a. aspect adverb: 3, 7, 8, 9, 11 and 12 (Line 12 is a rather special case as it is used with a positive verb, but the meaning is 'you're not going to die yet'.)
b. linking adverb: 1, 2, 14, 17 and 18; on 1 and 2, *and* is the conjunction

c. conjunction: 13, 15, 19 and 20
d. part of *be/have yet to*: 4 and 5
e. emphasising a greater degree or larger amount: 6 and 10
f. contrasting two adjectives: 16

Activity 6.3

a. The tense on all the lines is present perfect, apart from examples of the present tense (lines 6, 7 and 12) and past tense (line 10). On line 9 no tense is mentioned, but the present can be assumed.
b. The position is middle on every line apart from line 9, where there is no subject or verb.

Activity 6.4

a. with a noun phrase: 1, 2, 3 and 12
b. with a verb phrase: 11
c. before a comparative: 6, 7, 8, 9 and 10 (*Note:* line 7 has *more* as a determiner, but it should be included in this group.)
d. as part of a conjunction: 4 and 5

Activity 6.5

a. adjective: 3, 7, 12 and 13
b. expression: 4 (*not only…but also*) and 11 (*if only*)
c. adverb:
   1. *a few paces*
   2. *amenity purposes*. Note that *only* comes after the element it is referring to.
   5. *if the threshold test is met*
   6. *on Saturday*
   8. *for those…*.
   9. *a wheeze*
   10. *when there is…*
   14. *very few*
   15. *when the spirit…* Note the **inversion** ('is it') that follows from using *only* at the start of the clause.

Only could be moved on lines 1, 2, 5, 6, 9, and 10.

Activity 6.6

a. unusual position: 4
b. The previous sentences probably state:
   1. the institute will do other things
   2. the setting can be selected by other means
   3. there will be non-contemporary masks
   4. it is open to the women
   5. the table demonstrates other things

6. older tests are described
7. there are implications for other policies
8. other services are planned
9. it does other things, perhaps importing spirits
10. he wrote other types of music

Activity 6.7

a. comment adverb: 1, 2, 3, 4, 6, 7 and 8
b. central adverb: 5

Activity 6.8

There is only one degree adverb: line 5. On lines 2, 8 and 10 commas could be added in writing to separate *however* and to make its linking function clearer.

Activity 6.9

a. central adverb: 1, 4, 5 and 6
b. comment adverb: 2, 3, 7, 8, 9 and 10. Lines 7 and 9 could conceivably be central adverbs.

Activity 6.10

a. central adverb: 4, 6 (both cases) and 8
b. degree adverb: 1, 2, 3, 5, 7, 9 and 10

Activity 6.11

a. degree adverb: 1, 2, 4, 5, 7, 8, 9, 11 and 12
b. adjective: 3, 6 and 10

Activity 6.12

a. degree adverb: 1, 3, 4 (both cases), 5, 7, 9 and 10. Note that *much* and *many* are treated as adjectives here.
b. focussing adverb: 2, 6 and 8

Chapter 7 – Verb patterns
Activity 7.1

a. auxiliary: 3, 7 and 10 (*have got*)
b. monotransitive: 1, 2 (second example), 4, 5 and 9
c. link transitive: 6
d. *have to*: 2 (first example) and 8

Activity 7.2

a. monotransitive: 1 (second example), 2, 3, 4, 5, 6, 10, 11 and 12. On lines 2, 6 and 10 the object precedes *do*.
b. auxiliary: 1 (first example), 8 and 9

On line 7, *do* is used intransitively; there is no object, even an implied one. The meaning is somewhat unusual: how things 'turn out'.

Activity 7.3

a. intransitive: 2, 7, 10, 11, 12 and 15. Only on lines 2, 10 and 11 does it refer to the physical movement.
b. monotransitive: 1, 3, 4, 5, 6, 8, 9, 13 (both examples) and 14. On lines 3, 6 and 9 the meaning is not 'manage'/'organise'. Lines 1, 3, 6 and 8 are passives.

Lines and 3 (*run over*) and 15 (*run along*) contain phrasal verbs.

Activity 7.4

a. monotransitive: 1, 2, 4, 5 and 8
b. ditransitive: 3 and 7
c. adjective: 6

Lines 7 and 8 are passives, so 'objects' have become the subject.
Lines 1, 2 (*set aside*) and 8 (*set up*) contain phrasal verbs.

Activity 7.5

a. monotransitive: 2, 3, 4, 6, 12, 15, 16 and 17. Note on line 16 the object (*an announcment*) precedes *make*.
b. link transitive: 1, 5, 7, 8, 9, 11, 13, 14 and 18
c. ditransitive: 10. Note that this can be related to make a pot of coffee for me.

Activity 7.6

a. link: 1, 3, 4 and 12
b. monotransitive: 2, 5, 6, 7 and 10
c. link transitive: 8, 9 and 11

Activity 7.7

a. monotransitive: 1, 2, 8, 10, 11
Note on line 11 that the object (*time*) precedes *give*.

b. ditransitive: 3, 4, 6, 7, 9, 12, 13, 14 and 15
On line 5 there is no object. However, there is an implied object: 'blood'.

Activity 7.8

a. ditransitive: 4, 5, 6, 7, 9, 10, 11, 12, 13, 14 and 15. On lines 13 and 15 one of the objects precedes the verb (cf. ...*only you can tell us whether*...; *They don't tell you what's important*).
b. monotransitive: 1, 3 and 8. On line 3 the object (*what grand stories*) precedes the verb; on line 8 *me* is an indirect object.

On line 2 *tell* is intransitive.

Activity 7.9

a. monotransitive: 3 (direct object), 6 (indirect object) and 7 (direct object)
b. ditransitive: 1, 8, 9 , 10, 11 and 12. In 8 the direct object (*the sort of question*) precedes *ask*.
c. *ask for*: 2, 4 and 5. In 4 there is also an indirect object (*her boss*).

Activity 7.10

a. intransitive: 1, 2 (a phrasal verb), 3 and 4
b. monotransitive: 5, 6, 7 and 8

Activity 7.11

a. intransitive: 1, 2, 6 and 9. Note the inversion on line 1; *a tiny settlement* is the subject.
b. monotransitive: 3, 5, 10, 11 and 12. On line 12 the implied object (*they*) precedes grow.
c. link: 4, 7 and 8

Activity 7.12

a. link: 1, 2, 3, 5, 6 and 12
b. monotransitive: 4, 7, 8, 9, 10 and 11

Chapter 8 – Modal auxiliaries

Activity 8.1

a. possibility: 1, 2, 4, 6, 11 and 12
b. permission: 9
c. ability: 3, 5, 7, 10 and 13
d. request: 8

Activity 8.2

a. possibility, present: 1
   possibility, future: 2, 3, 4, 6, 14 and 15
b. ability, future: 9 and 10
   ability, past: 5, 11, 12 and 13
c. request: 7 and 8

Activity 8.3

a. possibility: 1, 2, 3, 5, 6, 7 and 8 (note *may have* + *-ed* participle, referring to past time), 9, 11, 12, 14 and 15
b. permission: 4, 10, 13 (both). On line 13 the first example is potentially ambiguous, but the second example makes it clear.

Activity 8.4

All the lines refer to possibility (including a past possibility which did not eventuate with *might have* on lines 4 and 5). This reflects their relative frequency.

Activity 8.5

a. all refer to future time
b. intrinsic: 1, 4 and 6
   extrinsic: 2, 3, 5, 7, 8, 9, 11, 12, 13, 14 and 15

On line 10, it could be either, or rather, the two meanings are merged.
Note the two 'first conditionals' on lines 4 and 6.

Activity 8.6

a. explicit conditional: 1, 4 (second example), 7, 10 and 13. Only 1 and 7 are instances of the 2nd conditional.
b. implicit conditional: 5, 6, 9 (with *have*), 11, 12 and 15
c. future in the past (including reported speech: 2 and 3
d. past habits: 8 (both)
e. tentative statement: 4 (first example) and 14. Note that it is the second example on line 4 which expresses the conditional.

Activity 8.7

On the following lines *will* could not replace *shall*:

- 2, because this is formal, legal language
- 6, 7 and 12, because these are suggestions (In Irish English and other varieties these could be made with *will*.)

On the other lines *will* can replace *shall*.
Note on line 4 how *will* is used in the same context as *shall* – interchangeably, it seems.

Activity 8.8

a. obligation in the present or future: 1, 2, 6, 7, 8, 9, 10 and 14
b. strong probability: 3, 5 and 11
c. formal request: 4
d. past obligation which did not happen: 12 and 13

Activity 8.9

a. obligation: 1, 3, 10, 13 and 14
b. deduction: 2, 6, 7, 8 and 11 (note *must have*)
c. necessity: 4, 5, 9, 12 and 15

NB. Some of the lines can be interpreted differently, especially those in a) and c).

Activity 8.10a

a. a full verb : 1, 2, 3, 5, 6, 7, 8, 9 and 10
b. a modal: 4

Activity 8.10b

a. a full verb: 8 (possibly influenced by *bother to*) and 9
b. a modal: 1, 3, 4, 5, 6 and 7

Line 2 has elements of both: a negative **imperative** with *don't* (modals do not have imperatives) but a bare infinitive. Line 10 is unclear grammatically; it could be followed by *advertise* or *to advertise*.

Chapter 9 – Multi-word verbs

Activity 9.1

a. phrasal verb: 3, 8 and 10
b. prepositional verb: 1, 2, 5, 7 and 9. On lines 1, 7 and 9 it means 'attack'; on lines 2 and 5 it means 'depend on'.
c. verb + preposition: 4 ('turn on the slopes')

Line 6 is, of course, a trick: a noun + preposition.

Activity 9.2

a. phrasal verb:
5. (both cases; the particles *around* and *on* must follow the pronoun)
6. (the particle *on* is unlikely to be moved because there is a long object)
7. (you could also say *pass those benefits on to the customer*)
8. (*pass out* is intransitive. This is the only really idiomatic phrasal verb.)
10. (*pass through* is intransitive. This has basically the same meaning as 9 and 11.)
b. preposition + verb: 1 (the preposition *to* comes after the object), 2, 3, 4, 9, 11 and 12

Regarding line 3, there is actually a phrasal verb *pass by*, but this is not an example of it as *by* would have to come after the pronoun.

Activity 9.3

a. phrasal: 2 and 10
b. prepositional: 1, 3, 4, 6, 8 and 9
c. verb + preposition: 5 and 7

Note on line 8 the plural form of the verb *look* with the singular noun *union*. This is an example of a **collective noun**; see 1.0, 1.10 and 1.11.

Activity 9.4

look at (lines 1 and 2): prepositional
look away (line 3): phrasal (intransitive)
look for (lines 4 and 5): prepositional
look forward to (lines 6 and 7): phrasal/prepositional
look over (line 8): phrasal
look out for (lines 9 and 10): phrasal/prepositional

Activity 9.5

1. *put out*: phrasal
2. *put in*: phrasal (= 'enter')
3. *put in*: phrasal (= 'contribute')
4. *put* + preposition *into* (note this is a passive)
5. *put* + preposition *in*
6. *put* + preposition *on*
7. *put down to*: phrasal/prepositional (transitive)
8. *put down*: phrasal
9. *put back*: phrasal
10. *put* + preposition *to*
11. *put on*: phrasal
12. *put up*: phrasal

Activity 9.6

Set for on line 3 is a simple combination of verb and preposition. *Aside* on lines 1 and 2 and *up* on 7 and 8 are particles and can be moved after the object. *Set off* (line 4) and *set out* (lines 5 and 6) are intransitive phrasal verbs, so particle movement is not possible.

Activity 9.7

come about (lines 1 and 2): phrasal (intransitive, + preposition on line 1)
come across (3 and 4): prepositional
come back (5 and 6): phrasal (+ preposition on line 6)
come forward (7): phrasal (intransitive, + preposition)
come from (8): verb + preposition
come in for (9): phrasal/prepositional

come into (10): prepositional (= 'are involved in')
come into (11): verb + preposition
come off (12): prepositional
come on (13 and 14): phrasal (but with different meanings)
come over (15): phrasal (intransitive)
come to (16 and 17): prepositional (meaning 'reach' and 'end up in', respectively)
*come up _with_* (18): phrasal/prepositional
come up (19): verb + preposition
come with (20): verb + preposition

Activity 9.8

a. phrasal verb (meaning 'convey'): lines 1 (both examples) and 5. In 5 *yourself* is an emphatic pronoun (see 2.5) and so it is not an object.
b. prepositional verb lines 3, 4, 6 (meaning 'recover from') and 8
c. a verb + preposition combination: 2 and 7. On line 2, *over* means 'more than'.

Activity 9.9

a. intransitive single-word: 3, 6 and 8
b. intransitive phrasal verb: 1 (*go along*), 2 (*go back*), 4 (*go off*) and 5 (*go out*)
c. prepositional verb: 7 (*go through*)

Chapter 10 – Question words, relative words and subordinators

Activity 10.1

a. question word: 3 and 12
b. relative word: 1, 2, 4, 5, 6, 7, 8, 9, 10, 11, 13 and 14
c. subordinator: 15

Only lines 3 and 15 exhibit the determiner use; the rest contain pronouns.

Activity 10.2

question word: 2, 3 and 15
relative word: 1, 4, 5, 6, 8, 9, 10, 12, 13 and 14
subordinator: 7 and 11 (an object nominal clause in both cases)

Activity 10.3

a. *Who* could replace *whom* on lines 2, 4, 9 and 10 (though with a less formal tone). On all the other lines *whom* is preceded by a preposition.
b. On every line *whom* is a relative word. This reflects the rarity of its use in the two other ways.

Activity 10.4

a. question word: 7
b. relative word: 1, 2, 3, 4, 5, 6, 9, 10, 11, 12, 13, 14 and 15
c. subordinator: 8

Activity 10.5

a. question word: 1, 6, 8 (both examples) and 9 (All are pronouns apart from line 6, which is a determiner.)
b. subordinator: 2, 3, 4, 5, 7, 10, 11 and 12

The type of nominal clause that it introduces is:

c. subject: 7, 10 and 12
d. predicative: 2 and 3
e. object: 4, 5 and 11. Note that though 4 is a question, *what* is not a question word.

Activity 10.6

All are subordinators, and all introduce adverbial clauses, apart from line 15 (a relative word). Note that on lines 3 and 12 the questions depend on other words. And on line 13 there is a case of extraposition, where the *when* clause could be the subject of the main clause, replacing the dummy *it*: And when *you don't know what's going on is always a worry.*

Activity 10.7

a. question word: 1, 4, 9, 12 and 15
b. relative word: 2, 3, 7, 8, 11, 13 and 14
c. subordinator: 5 and 6 (both introducing an object nominal clause), and 10 (introducing a predicative nominal clause)

Activity 10.8

a. question word: 1, 4, 11, 12, 14 and 15. (Note that *why* in 15 has actually been converted into a premodifier of 'questions'.)
b. relative word: 7
c. subordinator: 2, 3, 5, 6, 8, 9 (both cases), 10 and 13. On lines 2, 6, 8 and 10 *why* introduces a predicative nominal subordinate clause; on lines 3, 5, 9 (both cases) and 13 it introduces an object nominal subordinate clause.

Activity 10.9

a. question word: 3, 4, 5, 6, 7, 8, 10, 16 and 19
b. subordinator: 1, 2, 11, 12, 13, 14, 15, 17, 18 and 20
c. part of an exclamation: 9

d. central adverb: 2, 6, 7, 8, 11, 12, 13, 14, 16, 17 and 20
e. degree adverb: 1, 3, 4, 9, 10, 15, 18 and 19

On line 5: *how about* does not fall into either category.

Chapter 11 – Multi-functional words (1)

Activity 11.1

a. a preposition: 3, 4, 9, 10, 11, 14 and 15
b. an adverb particle: 1, 2, 5, 12 and 13
c. an adverb postmodifying a noun: 8
d. a verb: 7
e. a noun: 6

Note that in 5 there is a transitive phrasal verb, so the particle can be moved: *...sending its poison print-outs round.*

Note that in 15 the meaning is 'near to'.

Activity 11.2

a. adverb particle: 1, 3, 8, 10, 11, 12 and 15. Note that on line 8, *back* could be moved to the end of the line after the object.
b. adverb: 4, 5, 6
c. noun: 2, 7, 13
d. adjective: 9
e. verb: 14 (a phrasal verb *back up*)

Activity 11.3

a. adverb particle: 1, 2, 3, 5, 6, 7, 11 and 12. In 1, 2 and 3 *down* could be moved as the verbs are transitive with objects. On line 7, although there is an object, it cannot be moved because the object is a pronoun (*that*).
b. adverb: 4
c. preposition: 9 and 10
d. verb: 8 (meaning 'drink')

Activity 11.4

a. adjective: 1, 2, 3, 7, 8, 9 and 12
b. adverb: 4 and 10
c. discourse marker: 5 and 6
d. noun: 11

Activity 11.5

a. discourse marker: 3, 7, 8 and 9
b. adverb: 1, 4, 5, 10 and 11
c. adjective: 6
d. expression: 2

Activity 11.6

a. adjective: 1, 2, 4, 5 and 10
b. preposition: 7, 9, 11, 12, 13, 14 and 15
c. noun: 3, 6 and 8

Activity 11.7

a. noncount noun: 1, 6, 8, 12
b. count noun: 5 and 9
c. adjective: 2 ('not heavy'), 3 ('not dark'), 4 ('not heavy') and 7 ('not serious')
d. verb: 10 and 11

Note that on line 9 *light* is a noun premodifying the head noun, *room* ('a room for lights'), and that on line 12 *a little* is a determiner, meaning 'a small quantity (of light)'; see Chapter 3, section 7.

Activity 11.8

a. preposition: 1, 2, 3, 4, 6 and 9
b. conjunction: 11
c. quotative: 5
d. verb: 7, 8, 10 and 12

Activity 11.9a

a. adjective: lines 2, 3, 4, 5 and 6. On line 2 it is part of a phrase *a little bit* which has the same meaning as the determiner *a little*.
b. determiner with noncount nouns: lines 1, 8, 10, 11 and 12
c. pronoun: 7 and 14
d. adverb: 9, 13 and 15

Activity 11.9b

Adding *a* changes the meaning to positive on lines 1, 7, 8, 10, 11 and 14.

Activity 11.10

a. noun: 2, 3 (first example), 5, 11, 15 and 16
b. (part of) an adverb: 1, 6, 7, 8, 9, 12 (both examples) and 14
c. an adjective: 3 (second example), 4, 10 and 13

Chapter 12 – Multi-functional words (II)

Activity 12.1a

a. demonstrative pronoun: 3, 5, 6, 7, 8, 11 and 12
b. demonstrative determiner: 2, 4, 9 and 10
c. degree adverb: 1

Activity 12.1b

a. relative pronoun: 2, 7 and 15
b. nominal clause: 3, 4, 5, 6, 8, 9 and 14. (All introduce the object of the preceding verb, apart from 12, which introduces the predicative.)
c. extraposition: 11 ('That the ....has become clear.') and 18 ('That women...is likely.')
d. complement clause: 10 (after *belief*), 12 (after *pleased*) and 13 (after *view*)
e. appositive clause: 17 ('the fact that')
f. *so that*: 1 and 16

Activity 12.1c

That can be omitted in most cases, though in some it does help to make the structure clearer. It is only obligatory on lines 2 and 14 where it represents the subject relative pronoun.

Activity 12.2

a. existential: 1, 3, 4, 6, 7 and 10
b. adverb: 2, 5, 8 and 9

As can be seen, existential *there* is more common than the adverb use, much more in fact than the lines demonstrate.

Activity 12.3

a. numeral: 6, 7, 8, 11, 12, 13, 14 and 15
b. formal personal pronoun: 1 and 9
c. substitute pronoun: 2, 4 and 5
d. time adverbial: 3 and 10

Activity 12.4

a. determiner with a count singular noun: 2, 3 (both), 5, 8, 11 (both) and 12
b. determiner with a count plural noun: none (unless *data* in line 9 is considered plural)
c. determiner with a noncount noun: 1, 7, 9 and 10
d. Answer: 4 (This use is not represented proportionately on the lines.)
e. adverb: 6

Activity 12.5

a. adverb postmodifying adjectives and adverbs: 1, 4, 5, 6, 7, 11, 13 and 14 (On line 11 it is part of a comment adverb: 'strangely enough'.)
b. determiner: 8, 9, 12 and 15
c. pronoun: 3 and 10 (Note the non-standard form *cos* = *because*.)
d. adjective: 2

Activity 12.6

a. linking adverb: 1, 2, 3, 4, 14 (first example) and 15 (first example). On these lines something earlier is implied.
b. intensifer: 6, 7, 8, 9 and 10 (Line 6 is slightly different as it precedes a determiner.)
c. proform: 12 and 14 (second example)
d. *so...as*: 5; *so that*: 11 and 13; *or so*: 15 (second example)

Activity 12.7

a. preposition: 1, 2, 10 and 11
b. reason conjunction: 13
   time conjunction: 7 and 16
   manner conjunction: 8, 9 and 20 (note the inversion in 8 and 20)
c. *as...as*: 3, 4, 6, 12 and 15
d. *such as*: 5
   as soon as: 14
   as though: 17
   as well (as): 18 and 19

Activity 12.8

a. conjunction: 7, 9, 11 and 14
b. preposition of time: 4, 5, 8, 10, 12 and 15
   preposition of place: 1 and 2
c. adverb: 3, 6 and 13

Activity 12.9

a. conjunction of time: 4, 7 and 9
   conjunction of reason: 3, 6, 13, 14 and 15
b. preposition: 1, 5, 8, 11 and 12
c. adverb: 2 and 10

Glossary and index

The list of entries below serves as both a glossary and an index of important terms and concepts referred to in the book. In this way it saves you from having to check in two places to find an explanation of unknown terms.

As a glossary it explains terms that are highlighted in **bold** in the text. These are terms that are relevant to a description of the words, but to explain them in full in the sections would disrupt the flow of the description. And very often these terms apply to more than one word, or even to more than one chapter.

As an index it helps you to find explanations of terms and concepts that are already described in the text (usually, but not always, in one of the Introductions).

abstract noun: nouns which refer to feelings and ideas etc. which are not accessible to the senses (as opposed to 'concrete nouns'). They tend to be **noncount**.

adjective: see 4.0

adjective complement: see 4.0

adverb: see 6.0

adverb particle: a term for words such as *in*, *up*, *out*, *back*, etc. which are used with **verbs** to make **phrasal verbs** such as *look up*, *hand in*:

I handed my homework in.

adverbial: one of the **clause elements**. Adverbials often consist of **adverbs**:

They disappeared quickly.

but they are frequently composed of **prepositional phrases**:

He walked into the room.

and they can even consist of a **noun phrase**:

I saw him the next morning.

They can also consist of a **clause**; see **adverbial clause**.
One test for adverbials is that they answer questions with *when*, *where*, *how* and *why* (*When did you see him?*). Adverbials can occur more than once in the clause and their position is fairly unrestricted.

adverbial (subordinate) clause: see 10.0

agency: see **agent**

agent: the person or thing that carries out an action; sometimes called 'actor' or 'doer'. It is not the same as **subject**, which is a more extensive, grammatical concept. Not all subjects are agents (e.g. 'I' in *I know*), and agents can be expressed in a number of ways (e.g. with a *by* phrase after a **passive**).

antecedent: see **relative clause**

anticipatory *it*: see 2.6

aspect: a feature of the **verb phrase.** In English there are two aspects: **perfect** and **progressive** (and the absence of either, for which the term 'simple' is used). The two can also be combined, which makes four possibilities, as in these examples:

simple: *I sing*
perfect: *I have sung*
progressive: *I am singing*
perfect progressive: *I have been singing*

These can be combined with another feature of verb phrases, namely **tense** (the above examples are all in the **present** tense).

aspect adverb: see 6.0

assertive and **non-assertive** words: words that are conditioned by the context in which they occur. A **non-assertive** context is where the existence of something is not claimed (or 'asserted'). The significance of this is that certain words tend to be used in this context while their **assertive** counterparts are not. Common **non-assertive** words are *any* and its compounds *anyone, anybody, anything, anywhere* (as opposed to the **assertive** *some* and its compounds):

Have you seen <u>anyone</u>?

Yet (as opposed to *already*) is also non-assertive:

He hasn't come <u>yet</u>.

as is *ever*:

If you <u>ever</u> lie, I'll hate you.

Typical non-assertive contexts include **negatives, interrogatives** and **conditionals**, as above. However, it is possible to be assertive in these contexts:

Have you seen <u>someone</u>?

This supposes that 'someone' exists.

attributive adjective: see 4.0

auxiliary: a **word class** whose function is to form **verb phrases** with **verbs**. They consist of the **primary auxiliaries** and the **modal auxiliaries** (see 9.0). They are sometimes included in the **word class** of **verbs**.

bare infinitive: see **infinitive**

case: a factor which affects the form of **personal pronouns** and **nouns**. The **genitive** case is recognised for the latter. Regarding the former, a distinction is made between the **subjective** case (*I, he, she, we, they*) and the **objective** case (*me, him, her, us, them*); there is no difference for *you* and *it*. The subjective is generally associated with the subject of clauses (*<u>I</u> dislike football*), but the objective, while denoting objects (*The students don't like <u>me</u>*), has a wider role; for example:

Me, I don't like dancing.

The **subjective/objective** distinction also affects *who* and *whom*; see 10.3.

central adverb: see 6.0

clause: a unit of grammar between phrases and sentences in size. Clauses are made up of various combinations of **clause elements**. We need to distinguish between two types of **clause**: full clauses, and **non-finite clauses**. Full clauses always have a finite **verb phrase**, a **subject** (in almost all cases) and other **clause elements** determined by the **verb** (see **verb pattern**).

clause element: the basic component parts of a **clause**. Five clause elements are usually distinguished according to their function: **subject, verb, object, predicative** (sometimes called **complement**) and **adverbial**.

cleft sentences: see 2.6

closed word class: see **word class**

collective noun: see 1.0

comment adverb: see 6.0

comparative adjective: a form of **adjectives** that is formed in writing by adding *-er* (or a variation according to spelling) or *more* ___, e.g. *fuller, more beautiful*. Comparatives are commonly used with certain words, e.g. *much bigger*. **Adverbs** may also have a comparative form with *more*: *more recently*. See also **superlative**.

complement: something that is necessary to complete the meaning and grammar of a phrase. For example, in *afraid of snakes*, the prepositional phrase 'of snakes' is said to be an **adjective complement**, and in *a belief in witches*, 'in witches' is said to be a noun complement. Sometimes complements are obligatory; e.g. *fond of cats*. (See Chapter 5 for more on the use of **prepositions** in complements.)

conditional: sentences containing an *if* clause **tense** which express a condition. Traditionally a 'conditional **tense**', using *would* (see 8.6), was recognised for English, but this is not justified.

conjunction: see 12.0

content word: see **word class**

conversion: the process of changing the **word class** (or sub-class) of a word, as, for example, when a word that is typically a **noun** becomes a **verb**:

They *machine-gunned* the whole place.

or when a **noncount noun** becomes a **count noun** (the reverse is also possible):

Give me *a milk*. (Milk is normally **noncount**, but here it is **count**.)

coordinating conjunction: see 12.0

count: see 1.0

definite and **indefinite reference**: a distinction between the type of reference that **noun phrases** have. With a **definite noun phrase** it is possible for the reader or listener to work out precisely to which one (or ones) the writer or speaker is referring. This is shown by the use of the definite article or *which* with a noun phrase or a definite pronoun such as *it*.

The city is overcrowded.
Which city is overcrowded? (a question about definiteness)
It is burning.

With an **indefinite noun phrase** it is not possible to identify the referent.

definite noun phrase: see **definite reference**

degree adverb: see 6.0

delayed determiner: the three words *all*, *both* and *each*, when, in addition to their uses as **determiner** (and **pronoun**), they appear in or next to the **verb phrase**:

> *The men have all downed tools.*
> *My friends are both coming to the party.*
> *They each asked for a salary raise.*

The effect of this is to postpone the information they carry. Compare *All the men...*, *Both my friends..., Each of them...*

demonstrative: the four words *this*, *that*, *these* and *those*, which can be both **pronouns** (*I like that*) and **determiners** (*This book is mine*); the latter are sometimes called demonstrative **adjectives**. They are called demonstratives because it is said they are used to 'demonstrate', or point to something. However, this need not be something in the physical environment; it can be abstract (*I like that idea*).

determiner: see 3.0

direct object: see 7.0

ditransitive: see 7.0

do support: the use of the primary modal *do* in the formation of **negatives**:

> *I do not know him.*

interrogatives:

> *Do you know him?*

and emphatic sentences:

> *I do know him, I can assure you.*

dummy *it*: see 2.6

-ed participle: a **non-finite** form of the **verb**, used in the formation of **perfect** forms (with the appropriate form of *have*), e.g. *he has gone;* in **passive** forms (with the appropriate form of *be*), e.g. *she was robbed;* and in **non-finite clauses**, e.g. *known for their strength...* Most past participles are formed by adding *-d* or *-ed* in writing (e.g. *hoped, jumped*) or one of the equivalent endings in speaking, but **irregular verbs** form their past participle differently, e.g. *sung, known, taught*. All regular verbs (and some irregular ones) have the same form for the past participle as for the **past tense**. It is sometimes called the 'past participle', which is misleading because it is not past in meaning, in particular with **passives**; it is other words that convey the past meaning.

ergative: see 7.10

exclamation: see **exclamative**

exclamative: a sentence pattern which begins with *what* or *how* in a phrase that is fronted (see **fronting**):

> *What a lovely garden you have!* (a fronted **object**)
> *How beautifully she sings!* (a fronted **adverbial**)

Its main function is to express a strong feeling: an **exclamation**.

exclusive *we*: see 2.2

existential sentences: see 12.2

extraposition: see 2.6

extrinsic meaning (of modal auxiliaries): see 8.0

focussing adverb: see 6.0

fronting: a process in which a clause element is placed at the start of a sentence in order to draw attention to it; no other change takes place. This is common with adverbials but can also happen with objects, as in this example:

That film I liked.

function word: see word class

future tense: see 8.5

generic adjective: see 4.0

generic reference: see specific reference

genitive: a noun case that is used to denote a relationship between two nouns. This relationship can be one of possession (*the man's dog*) but not always (*the team's victory*). The genitive is marked in writing by the use of an apostrophe followed by '-s' for the singular (*cat's*), and the addition of the apostrophe (*cats'*) for the plural. This distinction is not heard in speech. It is also called the 'Saxon genitive', 'possessive case' or referred to by saying 'apostrophe '-s'.

gradable adjective: see 4.0

head: the central part of the noun phrase. Typically heads are nouns, but this position is sometimes occupied by an adjective (*the poor*). It is the only obligatory part of the noun phrase.

imperative: a verb form or part which is the same as the infinitive and which serves to give orders and make suggestions and offers:

Have a seat.

Clauses containing an imperative do not have a subject but are still regarded as full clauses.

inclusive *we*: see 2.2

indefinite noun phrase: see definite reference

indefinite reference: see definite reference

indirect object: see 7.0

infinitive: one of the non-finite forms of the verb. There are two types:
- the bare infinitive, which consists of the base form of the verb alone: *run;*
- the *to* infinitive: *to run.*

The choice between them depends on the grammatical circumstances: some verbs, especially auxiliary verbs, are followed by the bare infinitive (*I can see*), while others take the *to* infinitive (*I want to see*).

infinitive of purpose: *to* infinitives which are used to express a purpose:

He did it to calm their fears.

It can be paraphrased by *in order* [to].

-ing participle: a non-finite form of the verb, formed by adding '-ing' in writing. It is used in the formation of progressive forms (with the appropriate form of *be*):

They are singing.

and to introduce **non-finite clauses**:

Realising the danger, they left.

intensifier: see 4.0 and 6.0 on **degree adverbs**

interrogative: a term referring to the structure used for asking most types of question. It either involves the **inversion** of **subject** and **auxiliary**, or the placing of a **wh-** word at the start of the sentence, or both:

Are you coming?
Who rang the bell?
What are you doing?

Interrogatives can also function as requests:

Could you open the door?

intransitive: see 7.0

intrinsic meaning (of **modal auxiliaries**): see 9.0

inversion: a term for the switching of two words or phrases to show certain grammatical functions. Typically inversion involves a subject and auxiliary. The most frequent use of this kind of inversion is to form interrogative sentences:

Are you coming?

Inversion can also be triggered by the **fronting** of certain **negative** and semi-**negative** words and phrases:

Never have I seen such a sight.
Hardly had we got home when the explosion occurred.

It also occurs in some **conditional sentences** without *if*:

Had we known this before, we would have acted sooner.
Were I to answer, much trouble would arise.
Should he come, I would leave.

irregular verb: see **regular verb**

linking adverb: see 6.0

link pattern: see 7.0

link transitive pattern: see 7.0

link verb: see 7.0

main clause: in a sentence with more than one clause, the **main clause** is the one in which the **subordinate clause** forms a part.

mandative subjunctive: a form of the verb which is used in **subordinate clauses** after **verbs** of advising, suggesting, proposing or recommending; the form is identical to the **infinitive**:

We recommend that he repay the money. (rather than *repays*)
The report proposes the buildings be closed. (rather than *is*)

It is usually found in very formal writing. Alternatives are possible with the expected verb form or with *should*:

We recommend that he repays the money.
We recommend that he should repay the money.

The subjunctive form is in fact the remnants of a much more extensive **verb** system from early English. In general, its use indicates an unreal state of affairs.

middle position (of **adverbs**): see 6.0

modal auxiliary: see 8.0

modality: a type of meaning (or rather meanings) that is expressed by **modal auxiliaries** and other groups of words, e.g. modal **adjectives** (e.g. *possible*), **nouns** (e.g. *likelihood*) and **adverbs** (e.g. *apparently*). Modality generally has the effect of qualifying the proposition (or central idea) in a clause: *I may come/I will come/I should come*, etc.

The meanings involved include permission, obligation, volition, possibility, ability, necessity and prediction.

monotransitive: see 7.0

multi-word preposition: a **preposition** which consists of more than one word; for example *in front of, in spite of*.

multi-word verb: see 9.0

negative: a **clause** that includes the negative word *not* and has a negative meaning, and involving the use of *do* **support** with full **verbs**. Thus, the negative of *I like him* is *I don't like him*. With **auxiliaries**, the negative is formed without *do*:

I haven't seen him.

nominal clause: see 10.0

non-assertive: see **assertive**

noncount: see 1.0

non-defining relative clause: see **relative clause**

non-finite clause: a **clause** which is incomplete because it lacks a **subject** and part of the **verb phrase**. Non-finite clauses are introduced by **infinitives**, **-ed participles** or **-ing participles**:

To know him is to love him.
Known for its beauty...
Walking down the road...

Non-finite clauses may contain other **clause** elements, such as **objects**, **predicatives** and **adverbials**.

noun: see 1.0

noun phrase: the group of words that go together with a **noun**. Noun phrases consist of a **head** (which is obligatory) and three other positions: **determiner**, **premodifier** and **postmodifier**, as in this example:

The [determiner] *tall* [premodifier] *man* [head] *with a camera* [postmodifier].

All the positions are optional, except that of the **head**. Thus, a noun phrase can consist of one word, particularly in the case of **pronouns**.

People hate me.

Noun phrases function as **subjects** (*people* in the example above), **objects** (*me*), **complements** and occasionally **adverbials**.

number: the choice between **singular** and **plural**

object: see 7.0

objective: see **case**

object predicative: see **predicative**

open and **closed word class**: see **word class**

particle: see **adverb particle**

passive: a construction in which the **subject** of a **transitive verb** is replaced by the original **object**, and the **subject** is deleted or placed in a **prepositional phrase** starting with *by*; the form of the **verb phrase** is changed:

> *The people <u>love</u> her.*
> *She <u>is loved</u> <u>by the people</u>.* (passive)

The passive is used when the **agent** is unknown or not mentioned:

> *The President has been assassinated.*

or when the **object** needs to be placed at the start of the sentence:

> *Hamlet? Wasn't <u>it</u> written by Shakespeare?*

or when a long **subject** is placed at the end of a **clause**:

> *He was killed by <u>a tall man wearing a hat and a dark brown overcoat</u>.*

past tense: the **verb** tense that is formed by adding '-ed' to the stem of **regular verbs** (e.g. *I thank<u>ed</u> him*); **irregular verbs** may form their past differently (e.g. *sang* from *sing*). See also **present tense**.

perfect: see **aspect**

person: a distinction between **personal pronouns**. Three persons are recognised according to their role in the act of communication:

- first, referring to the speaker or writer: *I, we*
- second, referring to the listener or reader: *you*
- third, referring to participants: *he, she, it, they*

Noun phrases are also characterised as third person, which affects the form of **verbs** when they are the **subject**.

personal pronoun: see 2.0

phrasal-prepositional verb: see 9.0

phrasal verb: see 9.0

plural: see **singular**

plural noun: see 1.0

possessive: this refers to the possessive determiners and possessive pronouns. The possessive determiners are: *my, our, your, his, her, its* and *their*; the possessive pronouns are *mine, ours, yours, his, hers* and *theirs*; for example:

> *This is <u>my</u> desk.* (possessive determiner)
> *It's <u>mine</u>.* (possessive pronoun)

See also **personal pronouns**.

'Possessive' is not an ideal term because these words do not only refer to the idea of possession (e.g. *my car*) but to a whole range of relationships between people and **nouns**, including the idea of **agency**, e.g. *my achievement* means something I achieved.

The possessive determiners are commonly called 'possessive adjectives', but this is inaccurate: they are not **adjectives**. The term 'possessive' is also sometimes applied to the **genitive** of nouns (the 'possessive case').

postdeterminer: see **noun phrase**

postmodification: see **postmodifier**

postmodifier: the last position in **noun phrase** structure, following the **head**. Postmodifiers may consist of **relative clauses, prepositional phrases** and so on.

predeterminer: one of the three positions (the first) in **determiner** structure. Thus, *all* in the **noun phrase** *all the many people* is a predeterminer, occurring before other determiners.

predicative: one of the five **clause elements**. It is the least common **clause element** and only appears in certain **verb patterns**. Predicatives are involved in a relationship of equivalence with something else in the clause, usually the **subject** (*He became a teacher/ It looks dark*), but also the **object** (*They painted it red*).

Accordingly, two types of predicative are distinguished: **subject predicatives** and **object predicatives**. **Subject predicatives** come after link **verbs** such as *be*, *become* and *seem* and can consist of a **noun phrase**, an **adjective** phrase or **clause**:

He seems a nice man.
She grew tall.
They are what we need.

Object predicatives are used with link **transitive verbs** such as *elect, paint, make* (in one meaning):

They elected her President.
They made him redundant.

predicative adjective: one of the functions or positions of **adjectives**; that is, when they are placed after *be* or a similar **link verb** and function as the **predicative** (see above) in a **clause**. There are a few **adjectives** that can only appear in this position (*he is asleep*); these are sometimes called 'predicative adjectives'. See also **attributive**.

premodification: see **premodifier**

premodifier: the position in **noun phrase** structure that comes between **determiner** and **head**. Typically it is occupied by **adjectives** (*a lazy man*) but **nouns** are also common (*a business teacher*).

preposition: see 5.0

prepositional object: a third type of **object** recognised by some grammarians (see also **direct** and **indirect**) which follows a **preposition** in a **prepositional phrase**:

They laughed at me.

Questions about prepositional objects are formed using *who* (*whom*) or *what*, as with other objects:

Who did they laugh at?

and they can become the **subject** in **passive** verb constructions:

I was laughed at.

They should be distinguished from **prepositional phrases** used as **adverbials**:

They laughed in a strange way.

This could not become a passive:

*A strange way was laughed in.

prepositional phrase: a phrase consisting of a **preposition** and following **noun phrase** (e.g. *on the table*). Prepositional phrases can function as **adverbials** in a **clause**:

I'll see you in a moment.

as a **postmodifier** in a **noun phrase**:

a man in a dark blue suit

as the **complement** of an **adjective**:

fond of children

or as a **prepositional object**:

He shouted at me.

prepositional verb: a **multi-word verb** consisting of a **verb** and **preposition**; for example:

They're looking after my house for me.

The **preposition** is part of a **prepositional phrase** which includes a **noun phrase**. What distinguishes prepositional verbs from purely **verb + preposition** combinations is the meaning, which is idiomatic. With *look after*, the meaning cannot be guessed from the two words. See also **phrasal verb**.

present tense: the unmarked of the two **tenses**, as opposed to the **past tense**. In most cases it has the same form as the infinitive (e.g. *want*) but inflects for the **third-person singular** (*wants*).

primary auxiliary: the three words, *be*, *have* and *do*, which, unlike **modal auxiliaries**, have a full range of **verb** forms and, in addition to their use as **auxiliaries**, can also be used as **verbs**.

proform: see 12.6

progressive: see **aspect**

pronoun: see 2.0, 3.0

quantifier: a number of words that can be **determiners** or **pronouns**, and which refer to a quantity, e.g. *all*, *some*.

reference: the relationship between words and what they refer to in the 'real' world (which also includes abstract and imaginary ideas). Two types of distinction are important in English: that between **definite** and **indefinite reference**, and that between **specific** and **generic reference.**

reflexive pronoun: see 2.5

regular and **irregular verbs**: two classes of **verb** according to whether the formation of their **past tense** and **-ed participle** is governed by rules (regular) or whether their forms have to be learnt individually (irregular). For example, *sing* is irregular because its past tense *sang* and *-ed* participle (*sung*) cannot be predicted.

relative clause: a **subordinate** clause which forms part of the **postmodification** of a **noun phrase**; they are a way of introducing extra information about it:

I have seen the film <u>which won the Oscar</u>.

They are introduced by a **relative pronoun**, which is placed next to its **antecedent** (the noun phrase to which it is referring):

I have seen <u>the film</u> <u>which</u> won the Oscar.

Here, *the film* is the **antecedent** and *which* is the **relative pronoun**.

There is a distinction between 'defining' and 'non-defining' relative clauses (also called 'restrictive' and 'non-restrictive'); for example:

The man <u>who was wearing a hat</u> was a robber. (defining = the only man)
The man, <u>who was wearing a hat</u>, was a robber. (non-defining, extra information)

relative determiner: see 10.0
relative pronoun: see 10.0
reported speech: words spoken by one person which are then passed on by another person, for example:

She said <u>she was happy</u>.

sentential relative: see 10.1
singular: one of the choices in the category **number** in English, as opposed to **plural**. **Number** applies to most **nouns** and the **demonstratives**; for example:

singular *dog* – plural *dogs*
singular *this* – plural *these*

The term is also applied to **personal pronouns**, for example to the distinction between first person **pronouns** *I* (singular) and *we* (plural).
specific and **generic reference**: a distinction that applies to the **reference** of **noun phrases**. Specific reference refers to a particular individual or particular individuals, while generic reference refers to the whole group or class denoted by the word. The distinction also applies to **personal pronouns** (see Chapter 2):

Have <u>you</u> been here before? (specific)
<u>You</u> can tell he's lying. (generic, = 'one')

subject: one of the five **clause elements**. All full clauses (except **imperatives**) must have a subject:

<u>A table</u> has four legs.

Subjects usually consist of a **noun phrase**, and come first in the clause, preceding the **verb**; the **verb** agrees with it if it is **third-person singular** (**present tense**):

<u>The doctor</u> want<u>s</u> to see you now.

Subjects are often said to express the **agent** of an action, but in fact they may express a number of roles; for example, that of 'experiencer': *<u>I</u> feel good.*
subject predicative: see **predicative**
subjective: see **case**
subordinate clause: a clause which is secondary in importance to **main clauses** in sentences. They often function as part of a **clause element** (e.g. **relative clauses**) or as one element of the main clause:

I'll tell you <u>when he arrives</u>.

Here, the underlined clause can either be the **object** (= 'this is what I'll tell you') or **adverbial** (= 'that is when I'll tell you').

Subordinate clauses also include **nominal clauses**.

subordinating conjunction: see 12.0

subordinator: see 10.0

that **clause**: a type of **nominal clause** which is introduced by the **subordinator** *that*. **That clauses** usually function as the **object** of a clause:

I said <u>that I was coming</u>

but they can also be **subject**: *<u>That he is coming</u> is general knowledge*.

third-person singular -s: a form of the **present tense** of verbs required after **third-person singular pronouns** and **noun phrases** functioning as **subjects**, e.g. *he sings*.

to **infinitive**: see **infinitive**

transitive: a term applied to **verbs** that are used with an **object**:

I <u>hate</u> beer.

Transitive verbs are divided into **monotransitive** verbs (one **object**, as in the example), **ditransitive** verbs (two **objects**) and **link transitive** verbs (an **object** plus an **object predicative**). See 7.0 for more on these. See also **ergative**.

verb: an **open word class**. The main features of verbs are:

- they change their form for the **third-person singular** (of the **present tense**), the **past tense**, the **-ing participle** and the **-ed participle**;
- they combine with **auxiliaries** to form **verb phrases**;
- they determine the presence of other **clause elements**, such as **objects** and **predicatives**. See **verb pattern**.

verb pattern: see 7.0

verb of perception: verbs which denote the senses: *see, hear, feel, taste, smell*.

verb phrase: the combination of **auxiliaries** (if present) with a main **verb**. Its function is to serve as the **verb** element in **clauses**.

wh- **words**: see 10.0

word class: a group of words that have similar formal characteristics. There is no complete agreement among grammarians on what word classes there actually are, but in modern treatments they may include **determiner** and **auxiliary** as well as the traditional parts of speech such as **verb, noun, adjective, adverb, pronoun, conjunction** and **preposition**. See the individual chapters for more on these.

Word classes can also be divided into **open** (**verb, noun, adjective** and **adverb**) and **closed** (**pronoun, conjunction, preposition, determiner** and **auxiliary**) classes, according to whether they readily admit new members or not. This distinction corresponds to another: that between **function** and **content words**. The latter (**open word classes**) tend to contain the main content of a message, while the former may also have a grammatical function.

yes/no **question**: a type of **interrogative** which can be answered with *yes* or *no*:

Do you like her?